THE SHOW BAND

Over 1,000 Ideas, Shows, and Tunes for the Marching Band

by

AL G. WRIGHT

Director of Bands

Purdue University

The Instrumentalist Co., Evanston, Illinois

COPYRIGHT 1957 BY

THE INSTRUMENTALIST COMPANY

Oct. 1958

PRINTED IN THE UNITED STATES OF AMERICA.

Dedicated to my dear friend and counselor

HENRY FILLMORE

"He Was The Greatest Showman of Them All"

Henry Fillmore 1881-1956

ACKNOWLEDGMENTS

My sincere thanks to the many band directors throughout the country who, because of their requests for the publication of such a book and through their contributions of show ideas, have made this book possible.

I am also deeply indebted to Gladys Stone Wright, my wife and fellow band director, for her constant help and encouragement, and for her assistance in the preparation of the manuscript.

TABLE OF CONTENTS

It is a pleasure for me to have this opportunity to recommend both the writer and the contents of this book to you, the reader.

I have known Mr. Wright for a number of years and have had frequent opportunities to observe his work, both in concert band and marching band areas. On all occasions, I have found him to be a careful workman who invariably presents a good show with the band, but who also insists on high standards of musical performance and emphasizes precise basic marching above all else.

A brief enumeration of the principal accomplishments of the author which so uniquely equip him as an authority in the field of the marching band will be quite in order at this point. Al Wright served as Director of Music at Miami Senior High School for fifteen years following his graduation from the University of Miami. During this period of time he built an outstanding band and orchestra program in that school. The band portion of the instrumental music program was kept balanced with emphasis on both the concert and marching bands.

Starting in 1939 when he was in his second year at Miami, Al Wright took his marching band to state and national contests and consistently received first division awards. This was the case until he left to accept the position of Director of Bands at Purdue University in 1954. His marching band at Miami accepted many invitations to perform at numerous functions in the United States and Latin America.

During the latter part of his tenure at Miami, Mr. Wright often served as marching band clinician. His appearances included clinics at the University of Idaho, Western State College of Colorado, Vander-Cook College of Music in Chicago, the University of Miami, Florida State University at Tallahassee, and the University of Michigan. He has continued and expanded his activities in this area since going to Purdue University.

This book on the marching band will provide for the band director an immense amount of material with which he can build his marching band shows, whether they be for the football field, the basketball court, or the street parade. Here the reader will find literally thousands of show "ideas." The author has made no attempt to set down step - by - step or note - by - note procedures, feeling that most band directors prefer to develop an idea to fit their own situation, thus exercising their own natural talents of imagination. The manner in which this volume has been compiled makes it not a simple text for the development of the marching band, but in reality a sourcebook of ideas — a vast fund of material — which should make it a standard volume in every band director's library for years to come.

Glenn C. Bainum
Director Emeritus
Northwestern University Bands

CHAPTER I

DESIGNING THE BAND SHOW

Style

An important factor in preparing a marching group for performances on a football field, on the street, or on the basketball floor is the development of a distinctive "style" which will set that particular organization off from other groups in the area. Such a "style" will give the band a personality and, if distinctive enough, will actually make the group recognizable to the spectators even though other means of identification are not evident.

"Style" is nothing more than the use of a number of singular characteristics or elements such as "foot kicks," "knee bends," "arm swings," "instrument chops," that can be developed by the band director. Once "style" is introduced into a band's marching procedure, it will develop from year to year, changing slightly as the new students pick up and modify the several style elements. As the band develops its style, it also develops its morale. Also, the urge to be "different" is universal and the group, therefore, will tend to veer away from style elements that are being used by other bands in the area, thus continuing to develop a "style" of its own that will become more and more unique from year to year.

Some of the elements of "style" are described in the following paragraphs. A director, by selecting from these ideas, can develop a basic "style" for his band.

Instrumentation as an Element of Style

The "traditional" marching instrumentation is to place the trombones in the front rank followed by the baritones and the cornets. Then come the drums in the middle, behind which we find the basses followed by the woodwinds. (See Illustration I - 1.) This, of course, gives the band a solid sound but tends to relegate the woodwinds to a secondary position in the rear of the band where they can neither hear nor be heard very well.

Illustration I - 1

Traditional Marching Instrumentation

	5	4	3	2	1	
			x			Drum Major
1	x	x	x	x	x	Trombones
2	x	x	x	x	x	Cornets, Baritones
3	x	x	x	x	x	Cornets, Trumpets
4	x	x	x	x	x	Drums
5	x	x	x	x	x	Basses-Horns
6	x	x	x	x	x	Saxes, Clars.
7	x	x	x	x	x	Clars., Flutes

The reverse of the "traditional" formation is sometimes called the "symphonic" marching order. Here we find the clarinets in front with the drums again in the middle but the brass picking up the rear. (See Illustration I - 2.) This gives a fuller and more "symphonic" sound, but tends to reduce the volume of sound.

Illustration I - 2

Symphonic Marching Instrumentation

	5	4	3	2	1	
			x			Drum Major
1	x	x	x	x	x	Clarinets
2	x	x	x	x	x	Clars., Flutes
3	x	x	x	x	x	Saxes.
4	(x)	x	x	x	(x)	Drums
5	x	x	x	x	x	Cornets Trumpets

1

```
6 (x)   x  ,  x   (x)   x      Cornets
                               Baritones
7  x    x    x    x     x      Trombones
                               Basses
8  x    x    x    x     x      Horns
```

Note: The basses are sometimes distributed down the outside files* (see circled positions). This permits the rear ranks* to see the drum major easier.

Some bands put their clarinets both front and rear, again with the basses and drums in the middle and cornets and trombones on both sides of the drums. This gives a so-called "reversible" marching formation. (See Illustration I - 3.) By simply executing a to-the-rear march, a counter-march is effected. This arrangement is feasible only with large marching instrumentations.

Illustration I - 3

Reversible Marching Instrumentation

Rank numbers	5	4	3	2	1	Drum Major × File numbers
1	x	x	x	x	x	Baritones Trombones
2	x	x	x	x	x	Cornets Trumpets
3	x	x	x	x	x	Clarinets
4	x	x	x	x	x	Drums Saxes
5	x	x	x	x	x	Basses Horns
6	x	x	x	x	x	Drums Saxes
7	x	x	x	x	x	Clarinets
8	x	x	x	x	x	Cornets Trumpets
9	x	x	x	x	x	Baritones Trombones

Sometimes instrumentation "by file" (rather than by rank) is used. (See Illustration I - 4.) This is a particularly effec-

* Files are the rows from front to back; ranks are the rows from left to right.

tive method when script writing is in the show or where the formations include many curved lines (umbrella, rainbow, snowman) which are more easily formed by going into these formations by file rather than by rank. In such a marching order, the clarinets would be in one file, the cornets in another, the trombones in another, etc. This marching order does not necessarily lend itself to a good sound.

Illustration I - 4

Instrumentation By File

Drum Major
×

	Saxes Flutes	Trombs Basses	Drums Basses	Cornets Trpts	Cls
	5	4	3	2	1
1	x	x	x	x	x
2	x	x	x	x	x
3	x	x	x	x	x
4	x	x	x	x	x
5	x	x	x	x	x
6	x	x	x	x	x
7	x	x	x	x	x
8	x	x	x	x	x

Interval and Spacing

The set up of the block marching band also is a contributing element of style. Some directors prefer a relatively long, narrow band, while others prefer a wider one or even a square formation. A few have been known to march in a triangular formation with very good results. (see Illustration I - 5.)

2

Illustration I - 5

Triangular Marching Formation

```
        ×                    Drum Major

      ×   ×                  Trombones

    ×   ×   ×                Trbs - Bars

  ×   ×   ×   ×              Horns

×   ×   ×   ×   ×            Trpts - Cors

×   ×   ×   ×   ×   ×        Hrns - Basses

×   ×   ×   ×   ×   ×   ×    Clarinets
```

On the football field, the wider the ranks are, the more effective the appearance will be. Many fine high school bands and some university bands actually march in company fronts which extend from sideline to sideline, thus making 20 to 30 in a rank, but only a few ranks.

For parade purposes, the width should rarely exceed eight persons or be less than four persons. The width/length ratio of the band should not exceed one to two (be more than twice as long as it is wide).

In setting up the interval between the players, the spacing of the files is usually the same as that of the ranks. Thus, a band marching 2½ yards between ranks would also march 2½ yards between files. This makes it easier for the marching members to maintain their alignment and spacing.

Smaller bands may wish to double the space between ranks as compared to that between files. This opens up the band and gives it more apparent size. Thus, a band marching 2½ yard intervals between the files could put a 5 yard interval between the ranks. This would make a very good appearance on the football field since the ranks would still coincide with the yard lines.

Length and Style of Step

The military or "normal" marching step is used by many bands and particularly by those using a cadence of 120-136 S. P. M. (steps per minute). Here the stride is between 24 and 30 inches long. The foot strikes the ground heel first. This is an excellent step for long parades. It produces a fine military effect when performed at a reasonable military cadence (120-128) and with precision. It is also perhaps the easiest marching step to use while playing, since there is a minimum of jarring the lip.

The "glide step" is a special effect used by some bands for slow marching numbers. It is rarely used on a parade or throughout an entire show since it is both difficult to execute and not particularly flashy. In the glide step, the toe is pointed and the foot slid along the ground without lifting the knee. The foot stops in position with both the heel and toe on the ground at the same time. Slight modifications of this step are very effective when used with a waltz. Coupled with "The Skaters' Waltz" an attractive "skating" routine will result.

The "knee-high" step is becoming more and more popular among bands everywhere. It lends itself well to the fast tempos (160-220 SPM) that are now being used on football fields and in basketball arenas. The step is performed by raising the knee and pointing the toe. The knee should be raised until the thigh is horizontal. The toe remains pointed as the foot is brought down and the toe strikes the ground first. The length of stride should be shortened to at least 22 inches when using this step. A uniform "lift" of the foot is difficult to obtain among the bandsmen.

On the football field most bands use eight steps between five-yard lines (22½" steps), however, some prefer the longer six steps (30" steps) between yard lines, or to disregard the yard lines entirely.

In setting a "style," the most important thing is to obtain uniformity, whether you are using the high step, glide step, or a military step. Uniformity is the essence of style. A band that attempts to use style elements without uniformity or precision will make a sloppy appearance on the field.

Use of the Half-Time Formula

Many directors use a formula when building their shows. This is certainly a recommended technique. Quite often this formula becomes a point of departure, but it does establish a framework within which the director can work. In general, the following formula will provide a good start in building a show.

Half-Time Show Formula

1. Entrance
2. Fanfare
3. Pass in Review
4. Salute to the Participating Schools
5. Specialty of the Week
6. Finale
7. Exit

1. Entrance - Use the same entrance for each show. Get the band on the field quickly. Many directors prefer not to play on the entrance but use drums only. This allows the band to enter at a snappy cadence, and since there is no playing, the musicality of the performance is not endangered. This also allows the bandsmen to devote their attention to "style" by concentrating on their hand swings, instrument chops, and leg kicks.

2. Fanfare - Keep it short, snappy, and solid! This is a good place to bring the solo twirler and the majorette corps on the field.

3. The Pass in Review - Here the entire band parades down-field. Playing an introduction and two strains of a march. Use the same music every week. It will soon become a "theme" or musical signature for the band. The same principle is used on radio and television shows. The formation of the band in the "pass in review" can be either a regular marching formation or it can be in a company front. A HI or floating HELLO formation is always well received by the audience. Whatever "pass in review" is used at one game should be continued throughout the season.

4. Salute to the Two Schools - If letter formations are used for the school salute, move quickly in and out of the formations. If the school songs are used, play only one chorus. Try to get action into the formations by revolving the letters, (See Illustration I - 6.) Or, use simple dance steps while in the formations.

Illustration I - 6

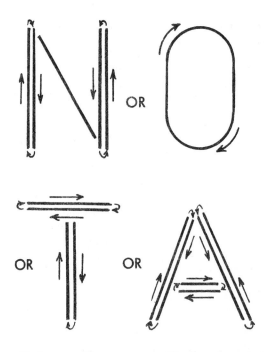

It is sometimes more effective to use a tune other than the regular school song with a formation. Many schools have "original" tunes that only their own supporters will recognize. A novel approach is to use something that pertains to the visiting school's nickname. "Tiger Rag" could be used when the "Tigers" visit; "Doggy in the Window" for the "Bull Dogs"; or "Black Magic" for the "Red Devils."

5. Special Maneuver, Skit, or Novelty - This is the high point of the show and should appear just prior to the finale. This part of the show should be different at each home game. It should also be timely, interesting, and enthusiastically performed.

6. Finale - Build the show to a climax or an ending, don't let it just run down. In some way signal to the audience that the show is completed with a closing harmonic cadence or a big tonic chord. This invariably brings forth considerable applause.

7. Exit - The band should leave the field quickly. Many directors float the last formation off the field and across the sidelines using only the drums playing the same fast cadence that was used for the entrance.

Types of Half-Time Shows

There are several types of shows currently being used by bands throughout the country. Many directors combine elements from the several show types in order to give their own performances . more spectator interest and contrast. Some of these types are described in the following section.

The Maneuver Type Show—These shows are most effective for use with low bleachers since they do not use formations to great extent. An impressive maneuver type show would include a drill type maneuver, letter salute, a dance step, and a simple formation. Almost a complete change of show can be effected from week ᵗo week by changing only the music and the letter formation.

In the maneuver type show, there is much emphasis on precision drill material. This type of work requires more time to prepare than formations or straight marching movements. Adjustments of rehearsal and drill time should be made accordingly.

The Theme Show — Here the music, action, and formations are combined with a good script read over the P. A. system to tell a story or otherwise develop an idea or theme. The script is very important and must be carefully written in order to tell the story in a few well chosen words and sentences.

When using the theme type show, it is necessary to present a completely new idea at each home-game show, together with new formations and new music. Once the band members get used to the routine of locating themselves in the several formations comprising a show and in moving from one formation to the next, the rehearsal of the theme type show will not demand extensive rehearsal time.

Transitions from one formation to the next must be made quickly and smoothly. There are several ways of doing this. The first is by rank and here the players retain their place in their rank, and move from one formation to the next by rank. This serves to preserve the playing ensemble by keeping "like" instruments together. It is also relatively easy to chart since the drill sheets need only indicate the location of the several ranks instead of every individual.

If well executed, moving by individual ᵛanks makes a pleasing appearance to the spectators. Going into formations by rank also makes it easy to substitute players in the event of sickness or for some other reason. There will be an experienced player on each side of the substitute. These players who know the formations can show the substitute where to go and otherwise serve as guides for him.

Then there is the "scatter" system. Here each player marches directly from where he is in one formation to where he belongs in the next. The scatter system is the quickest way to make formations since every player travels by the shortest route. Much care must be exercised by the director when charting his formations. First of all, the placement of the instruments in each formation must be such that they are in a position to provide a good playing ensemble at all times. Also, it is necessary that each player travel the shortest possible distance between formations. In charting, it is necessary to indicate every individual in every formation.

5

When going into formations by file, one or more players lead the entire band into the formation in file order. This is one of the slowest ways of making a formation. However, by utilizing the flowing lines formed by the files in motion, an attractive effect can be produced. The file system is the basic system used in "script writing." It is excellent for formations using curved lines.

The Pageantry Show—In pageantry type shows, the show is built by the movement of groups and blocks of people rather than by outlines formed by the band making various formations. In pageantry, the band can be split into two or more groups for variety. Also, blocks of majorettes, the school chorus, or even outside groups like Boy Scouts, cheer leaders, and student council representatives may be used. The effect desired is to achieve a "balanced pattern" on the field rather than to make formations which represent a thing or a letter.

The musical content and performance in a pageantry show is very important. Much contrast in changes of tempi is desirable. Quick-step marches, grand marches, waltzes, ballads, and musical comedy tunes can all be used very effectively. Here, too, is the place to use elaborate props, floodlights, soloists, blacklight effects, fire batons, streamers, and many other items to catch the attention of the audience.

Show "Building Blocks"

An outline of some of the many show-building devices is in order at this point.

A show sequence or idea can be built around any single one of these devices. A combination of several of these "tricks" will assure an interesting show.

I. Special Marching Maneuvers or Movements
  a) Flank Movements
  b) File Movements
  c) Rank Movements
  d) Scatter Movements
  e) Criss-cross
  f) Ripples
  g) Waves
  h) Freezes

II. Special Step Effects
  a) Kicks
  b) Goose Steps
  c) Side Steps
  d) Backward Marching
  e) Dance
    1) Waltz
    2) Swing
    3) Rumba
    4) Samba
    5) Charleston
  f) Squat (Dip)
  g) Tip Toes
  h) Skip
  i) Peg-leg
  j) Trot
  k) Run
  l) Shuffle
  m) Glide
  n) Lodge Drills
  0) Swing Drills
  p) Flash
    1) Instrument chops
    2) Hand Flash
    3) Hat Lifts
    4) Bows
  q) Processionals

III. Field Formations

  a) Letters and words
    1) Single line
    2) Double line
    3) Block — mass
    4) Script
    5) Moving or revolving
    6) Floating

  b) Designs
    1) Emblems
    2) Pictures
    3) Geometrical
      a. Squares
      b. Circles
    3) Balanced field composition

  c) Objects, standing still and animated
    1) Things
    2) Animals
    3) People

IV. Pageants

  a) Themes
    1) Dated (Gay Nineties)

2) Local Atmosphere (New School)
3) Patriotic (July 4th)
4) Occasional (Red Cross)
5) Interpretation of Music ("Rhapsody in Blue")
6) Historical (Paul Revere)
7) National (Thanksgiving)
8) Musical Comedy ("South Pacific")
9) Motion Picture ("Quo Vadis")
10) Carnival (Circus)

b) Participants
1) Bands
2) Drill Teams
3) Physical Ed. Classes
4) Clubs
5) Student Council
6) Glee Clubs
7) Majorette Corps
8) Boy Scouts
9) National Guard

c) Properties (Props)
1) Streamers
2) Festoons
3) Balloons
4) May Poles
5) Floats
6) Lights
   a. Hat
   b. Foot
   c. Uniform body
   d. Instruments
   e. Floods
   f. Spots
   g. Strings
7) Shakers
8) Vehicles
9) Umbrella
10) Flowers
11) Pigeons
12) Barrels
13) Platforms
14) Trees
15) Beach Balls
16) Fireworks
   a. Flares, Railroad
   b. Sparklers
   c. Roman Candles
   d. Fountains
   e. Rockets
   f. Fire Batons

d) Costumes
1) Sashes
2) Hats
3) Cloth Squares
4) Aprons
5) Chorus Robes
6) Old-time dress up

7) National groups
   a. Indian
   b. Dutch
   c. Irish
   d. Chinese
8) Fashion Shows
   a. Flapper days
   b. Bathing Suits
   c. Sports Togs
   d. New and old band uniforms
   e. Home Ec. products

Selection of Music for the Marching Band

Good music for the marching band is not necessarily difficult music. It is a mistake to select music that is too difficult for a band to play well. An easy march well played will sound better than a difficult march played poorly.

It's not good showmanship to play an entire march all the way through unless it fits a special routine being used. An introduction and two strains of a standard march is usually just about the right length. If additional music is necessary, use a drum interlude and go into another march. This second march should be selected with a good contrast of style, key, and meter (2/4 to 6/8 to 2/4). Select a march in which the range is moderate. Quite often notes that can be played relatively easily while seated in the rehearsal hall are difficult to produce while marching.

From time to time it might be necessary for a director to arrange music for his band. With so many fine arrangements for marching now being published, this should not be done any more frequently than is absolutely necessary. Arranging and copying parts take a great deal of the director's time that could be spent to better advantage rehearsing.

Where it is essential that the director arrange a tune, the "bob-tail" arrangements are recommended. These are commonly known as "five-way" or "six-way"

(Band-ette) arrangements. It is a good idea to obtain permission from the copyright owner before arranging tunes that are copyrighted. In most cases, permission will be granted provided proper credit is given when broadcasting. It is not necessary to obtain permission to arrange music that is in the public domain (these are known as P. D. tunes). Folk tunes and tunes that are more than 56 years old are in this category.

Student Instruction Aids

One of the greatest time-savers in the preparation of a marching band for a performance is the placement of cue sheets or formation sheets in the hands of each student. Unless the band is quite small (less than 20), drill sheets invariably result in a saving of time; although, admittedly, it takes some time for the director to prepare the charts for distribution to the individual students. The drill sheets should include all the information necessary for the individual to perform his part of any given show. This will include the music to be performed, the signals to be given, the position of the individual in each formation, the direction he is to face, how he gets into and out of the formation, and the action to be executed.

Charting the Formations and Duplicating Music

The duplication of "the charts and music" will be another problem. It is not advisable to have the students copy their own parts or charts since too many errors invariably creep in. The "ditto" (spirit duplicator) method is an easy and inexpensive method to use since the stencil can be made with an ordinary pencil. However, the results are not permanent; copies produced by this method fade and are not waterproof.

The mimeograph process gives better results and is more permanent. However the stencils (even those pre-printed with the music staff) are more difficult to prepare. Best results can be obtained by using off-set paper masters which are as easy to prepare as the spirit stencils and cost less than the mimeograph stencils. The printing equipment for this process is rather expensive and is found in only the larger schools or in the offset print shops.

In an emergency, photostats or "ozalid" black line or photo copy prints can be made. However, these are quite expensive and should be used only as a last resort.

CHAPTER II

THESE ARE THEIR BEST

A compilation of shows submitted by directors of outstanding
high school and college marching bands.

IN A TOY SHOP
Emmitt Clem
Plano High School Band
Plano, Texas

Music
"Clock in a Toy Shop"
P.A.
Have you ever thought what
happens at night at the local five
and ten? Even though the doors
are locked very tight we can get
you in.

Band in block formation facing
stands. Go into Clock Formation
on music.

Music
"Clock in a Toy Shop"
P.A.
(As the clock is ticking).
The clock on the wall strikes 12
times, and has a smile upon its
face.
The toys begin to come to life;
strange things are taking place.

Animate hands and pendulum of
clock.

Music
"Sailing, Sailing"
P.A.
The dolls jump into the sail-
boats, off and away they go. They
sail around all over the store,
while the little toy horns all blow.

Band forms sailboat.
Move sailboat down field
16 steps and back.

Music
"Old Gray Mare"
P.A.
Every night about this time,
the tractors begin to run.
They work and play all over the
store, until their job is done.

Form tractor; animate treads
on music. At end of music go
back to band position.

Music
  "Parade of the Wooden
  Soldiers"
P.A.
  Dawn is near and the music
  fades.
  The last thing we see are the
  soldiers on parade.

Band marches off field using
peg-leg (stiff leg) step.

THE BAND ON PARADE
Stewart King
Tippecanoe High School
Tippecanoe City, Ohio

Music
  Fanfare
  Visitor's School Song

Entrance.
Form visitor's school letter

E

Music
  "Thunderer"
(or other march)

Perform precision
  drill as follows:

The Band on Parade
  Intro — Mark Time — Step off at #1 (1st strain)
    #1 Into Band formation on Home Side
    #2

123 R Flank and 16 paces forward
456 L Flank and 16 paces forward

    #3

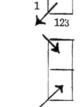

16 paces
Band Divides

16 Paces

    #4

Back in Band Formation

    #5

#6 Mark Time in Band Formation (Lift Feet)
 Majorette Routine

TRIO
#7 Countermarch

 1 2 3 4 5 6

#8 Countermarch
 Etc.

 6 5 4 3 2 1

Home School Song   Form home school letter

T

Show Band Formations by the University of Wichita Band
James Kerr, Director

IT'S WONDERFUL
Richard Bowles
Jefferson High School
Lafayette, Indiana

Music
Fanfare
P.A.
Presenting Drum Major Jerry Goddard (use your drum major's name) and the band.

Band in block formation at end of field.

Music
Any march
P.A.
none

Parade down field using oblique or other precision drill movements

Music
School Song

Float school letters down field.

JEFF→

Music
' 'S'Wonderful''
P.A.
The theme of the band's specialty this evening is "It's Wonderful."

Band forms football. Use majorettes for lacing.

Music
"You Gotta Be a Football Hero"
P.A.
First of all, the band thinks it's wonderful to enjoy the great game of football. Our formation is a gigantic football and the music, "You Gotta Be a Football Hero".

Music
"Let Me Call You Sweetheart"
P.A.
As the band moves into that heart formation, it's obvious that we think romance is wonderful. Now listen to some fine trumpeting as the band plays, "Let Me Call You Sweetheart"

Form heart. Have solo trumpet player play solo from center of formation.

Music
"Hail, Columbia"
P.A.
With the world in turmoil, it's wonderful to have friends and allies. As the band salutes our allies with the letters NATO, we hear the music, "Hail, Columbia".

Form letters NATO and stand fast.

NATO

Music
"No, No., a Thousand Times No."

P.A.
We interrupt our sequence to hear from the Russian delegation —"Mr. Representative, what do you think of NATO"

Form letters VETO and stand fast.

Music
'America, the Beautiful"

P.A.
If we start from the word VETO, we can get another word — a better word — just by transposing letters. Mr. Drum Major, let's switch the E with the O, and get a reminder for our duties on election day.

Form VOTE by floating the letter "O" into new position from VETO.

Music
School Song

Form traditional school letter.

THE THREE TREES
Richard D. Day
Little Cyclone Marching Band
Ames, Iowa

This show is built around the band novelty, "The Three Trees" by Tom McNaughton, arranged by Anthony Guerrera, published by Edward B. Marks.

The band marches out from the sideline into the "Three Trees" formation, as shown in Chart No. 1. Something should be used to represent a spring, as indicated by the circle on the 50 yard line. A sign may be used, or a small tub or wading pool partly filled with water, into which some dry ice has been placed.

It will be necessary to have this number directed from a podium at the sideline. There must be a narrator for the P.A. system.

Characters needed are a rabbit and a hunter appropriately dressed. Any small animal could be substituted for the rabbit, such as a bobcat, a tiger, etc.

Music
"Spring Song"

Band forms 3 trees. **Kneel.**
Place props in position.

Music
"Three Trees"

P.A.
Read script that accompanies the music.

As P.A. reads "Surrounded by the three trees, there — there and — there", one tree stands each time the word "there" is read. Costumed characters follow script.

Music

Any rock n' roll number.

P.A.

Ladies and Gentlemen:

We now present our version of this story with a modern touch. You see, there lived in this forest a tiger. He was a real cool cat.

Music

Jungle drum beat.

P.A.

One day some little Cyclones (that's us) decided to go on safari into the forest to capture the tiger, dead or alive.

Music

"Dragnet"

P.A.

Tiger character does short "rock" routine.

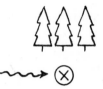

Six or 8 girls or boys dressed in your own old football uniforms, armed with rifles, baseball bats, etc., and wearing round safari helmets which are quite commonly worn in the summer by field workers. At the start of the safari music they march into the field toward the tiger.

After about 12 steps of this music or drumbeats, burst into the theme of "Dragnet." They pounce onto the tiger and put a rope around him. As the band plays "Tiger Rag," they lead him off the field, as the band assumes the opponent's school letter.

THANKSGIVING SHOW
J. Perry Watson
Appalachian High School Band
Boone, North Carolina

Music

"My Old Kentucky Home"

P.A.

The first home life was that of our settlers. It was a gay home where a fire was always burning and a welcome mat was out for visitors. The band salutes one of the pioneer homes where a good Thanksgiving dinner is probably being cooked right now.

Band forms cabin. Use CO_2 for smoke.

Music

"Home on the Range"

P.A.

Today's home is a far cry from the original log cabins which dotted the countryside. Nowadays, every man wishes to have a more modern home — with modern con-

Form Ranch House. CO_2 smoke.

veniences, such as television and the like. The band salutes a modern home where the family has probably gone out to a cafe to have its Thanksgiving dinner.

Music
  "Sailing, Sailing"
P.A.
  To many a person in the modern-day world, a home is a place oftentimes on the move. To many G. I.'s Thanksgiving dinner will probably be served on a ship at sea. The band salutes the service home of many service people.

Form ship. Use string of paper flags.

Music
  "Mighty Fortress Is Our God"

Form church or cross. Fill church with chorus people in white robes if chorus is available.

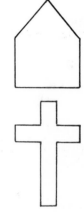

P.A.
  Not to be forgotten in this day and time is the home for all. You are cordially invited to join in with the band and sing a refrain of an old familiar hymn. The band wishes to express to you its best wishes for a Happy Thanksgiving.

DISNEYLAND, U.S.A.
James Kerr
University of Wichita Football Band
Wichita, Kansas

Music
  Fanfare
  "Men of Ohio"

Spread entrance.
Play fanfare in position and form block band on drum major's signal. March down the field and counter-march.

Music
  "Men of Ohio"

Block band . . . . .
Break from block band for first formation on drum major's signal. Continue playing march.

Music
"When You Wish upon A Star"

Compass . . . .
(Adventure Land)

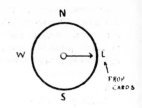

Music
"Air Force Song"

Rocket Ship . . . . . .
(Tomorrow Land)

Music
"Davy Crockett"

Coonskin Cap . . . . .
(Frontier Land)

Music
"Some Day My Prince Will
Come"

Castle . . . .
(Fantasy Land)

Music
"Mickey Mouse March"

Mickey Mouse . . . . .

Music
None
Band spells out Mickey Mouse,
and announcer fills in remainder.

MIC — See you next game.
KEY — Why Because we like
you.
MOUSE.

Music
Alma Mater

School letter formation

16

DECK OF CARDS
Peter A. Figert
Geneva High School Band
Geneva, Indiana

Music
"Let Me Call You Sweetheart"
P.A.
Bring out idea of love and
courtship.

Form heart.

Music
"Wedding March"
P.A.
Idea of marriage.

Form diamond.

Music
"Nobody Knows the Trouble I've
Seen"
P.A.
Family spat idea.

Form club.

Music
"Bury Me not on the Lone
Prairie"
P.A.
Burying the hatchet idea. Kiss
and make up.

Form spade.

MAGIC SHOW
Lester C. Eckart
Roosevelt High School
Kent, Ohio

Music
"That Old Black Magic"

Make hat formation

Music
"Here Comes Peter Cottontail"

Change hat to rabbit, or bring
prop rabbit (or costumed extra)
out of hat.

17

Music
Theme tune.
Music
Saw effect (snare drum).

Form stick figure.

Work prop saw.

Music
"I Ain't Got Nobody"

Separate stick figure.

THIS IS MY COUNTRY
James Kerr
University of Wichita
Wichita, Kansas

Music
"Yankee Doodle"

Spirit of '76.
Fife, drum, and American flag march down the field.

Music
"Yankee Doodle"

Block Band . . . . . .
At pre-arranged signal, the band enters and marches down the field.

Music
"Dixie"
Segue:
"America, the Beautiful"

Southern Flag . . . . .
(Civil War)
After bow, band breaks for this formation playing segue.

Music
"Battle Hymn of the Republic"

Northern Flag . . . . . .
(Civil War)

Music
"Goodby Broadway, Hello France"

Skyscraper . . . . . .
(World War I)

Music
"Over There"

Eiffel Tower . . . . . .
(World War I)

Music
"Nearer My God to Thee"

Religious Cross . . . . .
(World War II)
Iowa Jima flag-raising scene.

TABLEAU ↵

Music
"This Is My Country"

Shield . . . .

Washington State College Band, Pullman, Washington. Howard Deming,
Director of the Marching Band. Coonskin Cap Formation (See page 16)

19

AUTOMOBILE SAFETY SHOW
Peter Figent
Geneva High School Band
Geneva, Indiana

Music
"In My Merry Oldsmobile"
P.A.
Use safe driving idea.

Form auto.

Music
"Highways Are Happy Ways"
P.A.
40 M.P.H.

Wheels revolve.

DITTO

Music
"Nearer My God to Thee"
P.A.
60 M.P.H.

Wheels speed up a little.

DITTO

Music
"When the Roll Is Called Up
Yonder"
P.A.
75 M.P.H.

Wheels revolve faster.

DITTO

Music
"Lord, I'm Comin' Home"
P.A.
90 M.P.H.

Wheels speed up. Fly apart.
Auto smashes into pieces. Scatter
to next formation.

Music
"Taps," trumpet solo
P.A.
Safety message.

Tombstone formation

DANCE ROUTINE
"Alexander's Ragtime Band"
Al Riley
Technical High School
Fort Worth, Texas

Numbers denote measures beginning after the three pickups.   Take four steps per measure.

1	2	3	4	5
L TR R TL	SAME	SAME	LRLR	L TR R TL

6	7	8	9	10
L TR R TL	SAME	LRLR	LC LB	SAME

11	12	13	14	15
RC RB	SAME	LRLR	SAME	SAME

16	17	18	19	20
SAME	LT LH RT RH	SAME	SAME	LRLR

21	22	23	24	25
LT LH RT RH	SAME	SAME	LRLR	LK LD RK]

26	27	28	29	30
SAME	SAME	SAME	SAME	SAME

31	32			
SAME	LR Stop			

Legend:

LRLR ...One step each beat.
L ....Regular step with Left foot.
R ....Regular step with Right foot.
TL ......Tap left toe against right heel.
TR ......Tap right toe against left heel.
LC ......Cross left foot in front and to right of right foot.
RC ......Cross right foot in front and to left of left foot.
LB ......One backward step with left foot.
RB ......One backward step with right foot.
LK ......Kick left foot forward, waist high.
RK .....Kick right foot forward, waist high.
LD ......Left foot down to ground, either in a forward step
         or as in Mark Time.
RD ......Right foot down to ground, either in a forward step
         or as in Mark Time.
         The above may be used in parade or for football
         show.

A GIRL IN EVERY PORT
Carroll Copeland
Franklin High School
Franklin, Indiana

Music
"Sailing, Sailing"
or
"Anchors Aweigh"

Band entrance.

Music
"Peggy O'Neil"
(2 choruses)

Band forms shamrock.
Girl in Irish costume and sailor
do Irish Jig.

21

P.A.
   Announce dancers.
Music
   "Lady of Spain"

Band forms fan.
Girl in Spanish costume does flamenco type dance. Majorettes in line behind soloist do Spanish stomp type step.

Music
   "Can-Can" from
     "Gaite Parisienne"

Band forms Eiffel Tower. Soloist in ruffled Can-Can costume performs modified can-can dance. Majorettes back up soloist with similar steps.

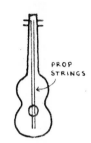

Music
   "Aloha"

Band forms Ukulele.
Soloist in grass skirt performs hula routine. Majorette line uses simple arm movements.

PROP STRINGS

Music
   "In a Persian Market"
   "Beautiful Princess Theme"
   (32 bars repeated).

Band forms oriental scimitar.
Soloist in Harem costume.
Majorettes seated do oriental head and arm movements.

Music
   "Cross Over the Bridge"
   or any American swing tune.

Band forms bridge.
Sailor Boy waves goodby to solo dancers. He crosses bridge and is met by U.S. girl and they do jitterbug or rock routine.

MUSIC DEPARTMENT ON PARADE
James Kerr
University of Wichita "Shocker" Band
Wichita, Kansas

Music
   "Sailing, Sailing"
    Segue: "Music, Maestro,
     Please"

Break from block band on drum Major's signal and form ship while playing segue. Mark time until end of segue. Halt on last note.

Music
  "My Bonnie Lassie"
P.A.
  Honoring the Band

Stick man with baton.

Music
  "Prelude in C# Minor"
P.A.
  Honoring the vocal department.

Piano

Music
  "Kuretzer 2"
    (Jack Benny's warm-up)
P.A.
  Honoring the orchestra.

Violin

Music
  "Scales, Chords, and Musical
    Exercises"
P.A.
  A day in the practice rooms.

Practice Rooms . . . . .

Music
  Alma Mater

School letter.

GLEN MILLER SHOW
H. G. Palmer
Fort Hays Kansas State College
Hays, Kansas

Music
  "Moonlight Serenade"
  "St. Louis Blues March"

Band forms moon. Move to next
formation on "Blues."

Music
  "Pennsylvania 6-5000"
  "St. Louis Blues March"

Band forms telephone. Move to next formation on "Blues."

Music
  "Chattanooga Choo-Choo"
  "American Patrol"

Band forms locomotive. Move to next formation on "American Patrol."

Music
  "Tuxedo Junction"
  16 bar drum cadence

Band forms road junction. Move to next formation on drums.

Music
  "Moonlight Cocktail"
  "American Patrol"

Band forms cocktail glass (or coke bottle). Move to next formation on "American Patrol."

Music
  "Little Brown Jug"

Band forms Jug.
EXIT

CORONATION SHOW
(For Homecoming or other Queen)
Richard Kucera
Ashland City Schools
Ashland, Nebraska

Music
  Drums

Form band at end of field.

Music
  School Marching Song
P.A.
  Announce Homecoming Show.

Parade down field. Halt center and face stands.

Music
"On the Square" March

Band forms hollow square.

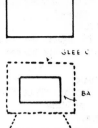

Music
"To Look Sharp" March

If available use Glee Club to form TV set around square. Or band put hats on ground to form squares then band forms TV set.

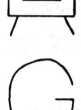

Music
"Let Me Call You Sweetheart"
"For He's a Jolly Good Fellow"
P.A.
Announce King and Queen.

On signal, band and chorus kneel. King and Queen enter from sideline and take places in **TV** set formation.

Music
Visiting School Song

On Drum Major's signal groups rise. Glee Club leaves field and band forms letter of visiting school

Music
Alma Mater

Form home school letter

Music
"Home Sweet Home" in bright march tempo.

EXIT

BAND MOTHERS' SALUTE
Charlotte Hickman
Pond Creek High School Band
Pond Creek, Oklahoma

Music
none
P.A.
The Pond Creek Band is dedicating its half-time show to the Pond Creek Band Mothers' Club. The Band moms were organized in the fall of 1940 and have been a dominant factor in the continued development of the band program in our school.

Band holds entrance position. Marchs down field after announcement.

Music

"That Wonderful Mother of Mine"

P.A.

To open the show, the band forms a big bonnet outline.

Form bonnet and hold position.

Music

Repeat, "That Wonderful Mother of Mine"

P.A.

And now a greeting to all of you Moms, and what could be more symbolic than a clothesline full of diapers?

Twirlers hang up diapers on clothesline. (Spell "Hello Mom.") Bring in gimmick of looking for the "O" diaper as you have "Hell Mom" on the line temporarily.

Music

"Rockabye Baby"

P.A.

Remember when you rocked us in a cradle and sang to us?

Form cradle.
Rock cradle.

Music

"School Days"

P.A.

And then came the day when you watched us start off to school and you knew that we were growing up. Of course we studied readin', 'riting, 'rithmetic, and **BAND.**

Form figures.

$1 + 1 = 2$

Music

"School Days"

P.A.

Look, Mom, we can read too.

Move to CAT formation on repeat of music.

Music

"Ma, He's Making Eyes at Me"

P.A.

And then we found out that we're boys and girls. No doubt you often wished we were back in the cradle.

Band forms heart and twirlers make the eyes roll. (Eyes are prop goo-goo style with movable eyeballs).

Music

"M-O-T-H-E-R Spells Mother"

P.A.

But really, Mom, we appreciate the many things you do for us.

As the P.A. system reads the words with the band accompaniment, flash cards spelling

Music
"Goodnight Ladies"
P.A.
And so now it is Goodnight Ladies and "Many Thanks to You"

Band in company front facing stands. Exit to sideline.

MARDI GRAS
Francis P. Comer
Canonsburg High School
Canonsburg, Pennsylvania

Music
"Old Man River"
"Here Comes the Show Boat"
P.A.
The High School Band has chosen for its show tonight a theme based on "Mardi Gras.

After forming riverboat animate paddle wheel and move formation down field.

Music
Waltz from "At the Circus" by H. Jones or "Merry - Go - Round Broke Down."
P.A.
In keeping with the Mardi Gras, the band illustrates a Merry - Go - Round. From every street children dressed in strange, gay figures wend their way and maskers dressed as monkeys and sailors prepare themselves to go to the carnival.

Use 20 foot center pole with twelve 25 foot streamers to form merry-go-round. Players holding streamers carry cardboard cut-out horses.

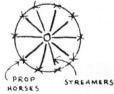

Music
"Can Can" #1 from Orpheus
P.A.
After a hectic day, the festive makers begin to fill the night clubs.

Band forms several circles representing tables (could be squares) Bandsmen kneel facing center. Majorettes perform routine in circles.

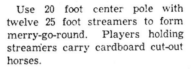

Music
"Old Man River"
P.A.
As the night of festivities ends, out on the Mississippi can be seen riverboats all lighted up and we can hear strains of "Old Man River."

Reform Riverboat. Use caplights in outline if night game.

27

COMMUNITY FUND SHOW
(Red Feather)
G. T. Gilligan
Kermit High School Band
Kermit, Texas

P.A.
Write announcements to suit local community fund situation.

Music
"That's Where the Money Goes"

Entrance.

Music
"I Believe"

Form word "GIVE"

Music
"My Friend"

Form word "TO"

Music
Any good march trio.

Form word "UNITED"
(this formation can be omitted)

East High School Band, Sioux City, Iowa. Dale Carris, Director
Carousel Formation for Mardi Gras Band Show (See page 27)

Music
"Pennies from Heaven"

Form Feather. Use red cap lights if it's a night game.

AMERICAN THANKSGIVING SHOW
J. Perry Watson
Appalachian High School Band
Boone, North Carolina

Music
Fanfare

Play fanfare while standing at end of field.

Music
"Onward Christian Soldiers"
(march — Al Hayes)

Play introduction standing. Step off at measure 9 and march to center of field. Form Mayflower, (boat formation). Face stands and halt.

Music
"America"

Play while standing in May-flower formation. Audience should join in singing. Step off and change to tepee formation (Tom - Tom cadence).

Music
"Indian Boy" (H. Bennett) or tom tom

Indian Dance — play while in tepee formation. Band members or others perform Indian Dance.

Music
"Church in the Wildwood"

Play introduction standing. Step off at measure 5 and change TEPEE to CHURCH formation and halt facing stands.

Music
 "Faith of Our Fathers"
 (march)

Play while standing in Church formation.

Music
 "God of Our Fathers"
 (march)

Play introduction standing. Step off at measure 52, four steps to the measure (4/4 March). Change CHURCH to CROSS formation and halt.

Music
 "Crusaders Hymn"

Play while standing in CROSS formation. Use brass only for organ effect, if such is desired.

Music
 "Onward Christian Soldiers"
 (march)

For Exit — turn back to (B) "Onward Christian Soldiers" and play introduction standing in CROSS formation. At measure 9, entire band must do a right or left face, and march down the field in the cross formation. Break formation on the 20-yard line, close ranks, and march off field.

"THE SAGA OF JAZZ"
Robert Warriner
William S. Hart High School Band
Newhall, California

Music
 Fanfare
P.A.
Football fans, for its half-time show this evening the Senior High Band will present . . . "The Saga of Jazz."

Move on to field.

Music
 "Basin Street Blues"
P.A.
The first tune you'll recognize as "Basin Street Blues."

Form trumpet. Segue to EIGHTH NOTE formation.

30

Music
  "Ja-Da"
P.A.
  From Lower Basin Street music, we move upstate to New York and with the Treble Clef formation the band will play the ever popular dixieland dance tune "Ja-Da".

Change to TREBLE CLEF formation.

Music
  School Song
P.A.
  Here is Hart's traditional block H and the "Fight Song."

Form school letter and EXIT.

"OUR HERO" Football Show
Tom W. Swayzee
Munford High School Band
Munford, Tennessee

Music
  Fanfare

P.A.
  The theme is designed to show facets of "Our Hero," the All-American football player.

Entrance.

Music
  "My Hero"

Proceed down field and into stick figure (man) formation.

P.A.
  Ladies and Gentlemen:
The Band salutes the hero of the season, the ALL-AMERICAN football player, whoever he may be to you.

Music

"You Gotta Be a Football Hero"

P.A. (over music)

Our football hero, as formed by the band on the field, can do many things well. He is an excellent passer. Hail to our passer hero.

Hold formation. Animate passing arm.

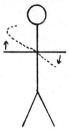

Music

"Football Hero"

(continued)

P.A. (over music)

Our hero is also quite a kicker. You see before you a picture of him in action. Notice the form with which he gets off those spiraling punts. Hail to the kicking hero.

Animate leg and arm.

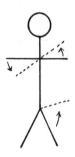

Music

"Football Hero" (continued) or segue to

"Mister Touchdown, U.S.A."

P.A. (over music)

Our hero is an excellent runner. His rhythm and grace are superb in the broken field. Watch for him through the season. He may break away anytime.

Add prop ball. Move figure down field ten or twenty yards, then break to next formation.

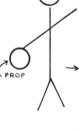

Music

None

P.A.

Our hero reaches the goal. For the school and the team he brings victory in the game. Our hero goes for the goal at every opportunity and will go on to greater goals in life.

Cut off music when goalpost is formed.

Music

"His Honor" March

Step off into TROPHY formation

Music
None
P.A.
Our hero shares in the winning of honors for his team and school. The trophy displayed on the field by the band reminds us of the honors and laurels that are his due. Hail the conquering hero.

Music
"My Hero"

Hold TROPHY formation.

EXIT

SPORTS SALUTE
Walter Welke
University of Washington Band
Seattle, Washington

Music
School Song
P.A.
Announce Band.

Band enters.

Music
"You Gotta Be a Football Hero"
P.A.
Script to salute football sport.

Band forms stick figure. Majorettes form ball on sideline and drop to position to meet rising foot of player. Ball is "kicked" down field.

Music
School Song or "Look Sharp March"
P.A.
Script to salute Basketball.

Form stick figure. Majorettes form basketball. Raise arms and toss basketball.

Music
"Take Me Out to the Ball Game"
P.A.
Script to salute baseball.

Form stick man with ball bat. Girls break into 3 small baseballs — go past the "Batter." The first two are strikes, the third a "hit."

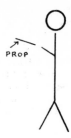

Music
"When It's Springtime in the Rockies"
P.A.
Script about spring and to salute track sport.

Form track shoe and jumping bar. Animate shoe over bar.

Music
"School Song"
P.A.
Script to close show.

Form School Letter and EXIT.

Ohio State University Band, Columbus, Ohio. Jack Evans, Director
Basketball player and basket formation for Sports Salute Band Show

CHAPTER III

ONE HUNDRED FOURTEEN COMPLETE BAND SHOWS

Air Age Progress
1. "Come Josephine in My — Old Bi-Plane
   Flying Machine"
2. "St. Louis Blues" — Lindberg
   Monoplane
3. "U.S. Air Force Song" — Jet Plane
4. (Rocket Effect) — Rocket

All Day Show
1. "Time on My Hands" — Clock Formation
2. "Reveille" — Clock Hands at 7 A.M.
3. "Oh, What a Beautiful Morning" — Clock Hands at 8 A.M.
4. "High Noon" — Clock Hands at noon
5. "Tea for Two" — Clock Hands at 4 P.M.
6. "Dark Town Strutter's Ball" — Clock Hands at 9 P.M.
7. "Three O'Clock in the Morning" — Clock Hands at 3 A.M.
8. "Good Night Sweetheart" — Clock Hands at 4 A.M.

Animal Show
1. "Tiger Rag" — Tiger and Ringmaster
2. "Bunny Hop" — Rabbit or Ears
3. "Doggie in the Window" — Dog in Square
4. "Hot Canary" — Bird

Armed Forces Day
1. Air Force — Plane or Wing
   "U.S. Air Force Song" — Insignia or USFA
2. Marines — Fouled Anchor or Ship (LST
   "Marines Hymn" — or USM)
3. Navy — Anchor or
   "Anchors Aweigh" or — Ship or
   "Sailing, Sailing" — USN
4. Coast Guard — Buoy
   "Semper Paratus"
5. Army — Tank or
   "Caisson Song" — Cannon or
   "There's Something — Gun or
   about a Soldier" — USA
   "You're in the Army
   Now"

Bachelor Show
1. "Standing on the Corner — Face with
   Watching All the Girls — moving prop
   Go By" — eyes
2. "Wedding Bells Are — Bell
   Breaking Up that Old
   Gang of Mine"
3. "Let Me Call You — Heart
   Sweetheart"
4. "Here Comes the Bride" — Church
5. Reprise "Standing on the — Exit
   Corner"

Back to School
1. "Hear Dem Bells" or — Bell or
   "School Days" — Schoolhouse
2. "An Apple for the — Apple
   Teacher"
   "Big Apple"
3. "Johnny Got a Zero" — Zero
4. "Tea for Two" — Lunchpail
5. " 'A' You're Adorable" — ABC Card or Slate
6. "When Day Is Done" — Clock at 3 P.M.

Bell Show
1. "Liberty Bell March" or — Entrance
   "Hear Dem Bells"
2. "Bells Are Ringing for — Bell
   Me and My Gal"
3. "Bells of St. Mary's" — Cross or Steeple

Bull Fight
1. "Paso Doble" — Bull Ring (Circle)
2. "Toreador Song" (Carmen) — Sousaphone Player (Bull) and Drum Major do bullfight business.
3. "Ferdinand the Bull" — Toreador wins with flowers

Calendar
1. "It's June in January" — Calendar with prop names "January"
2. "April Showers" — "April"
3. "June Is Bustin' Out — "June"
   All Over"

4. "September Song"	"September"
5. "Autumn Leaves"	"October"
6. "Jingle Bells"	"December"

Calendar of Sports

1. Spring	Bat and Ball
"Take Me Out to the Ballgame	(Majorettes with ball, bats, and caps)
2. Summer	
"Row, Row, Row Your Boat"	Boat or Fishing Rod
"Small Fry"	
3. Fall	
"You've Got to Be a Football Hero"	Goalposts
4. Winter	
"Skater's Waltz"	Ice Skate

Cartoonland

1. "Who's Afraid of the Big Bad Wolf"	Wolf
2 ."Heigh-Ho, Heigh-Ho"	Pick
3. "Mickey Mouse March"	Mouse Ears

Chinese Show

1. "Chinatown"	Pagoda
2. "Limehouse Blues"	Junk
3. "Chinese Temple Garden"	Chinese Gate

Christmas

1. "White Christmas"	Christmas Tree
2. "Onward Christian Soldiers"	Cross
3. "Adeste Fidelis"	Cathedral Window
5. "Jingle Bells"	Sleigh
6. "O Little Town of Bethlehem"	Star

Christmas Around the World

1. America	
"Jingle Bells"	Shield
2. England	
"God Rest Ye Merry Gentlemen"	Wreath
3. France	
"March of the Three Kings"	Camel
4. Germany	
"O Tannenbaum"	Fir Tree
5. Russia	
"Troika"	Sleigh
6. Hawaii	
"Aloha Oe"	Palm or Exit

Clock Show

1. "Time on My Hands"	Clock
2. "As Time Goes By"	Move Hands
3. "The World Is Waiting for the Sunrise"	6:00 A.M.
4. "Great Day"	Noon
5. "In the Evening by the Moonlight"	6:00 P.M.
6. "Rock Around the Clock"	Revolve Hands

Circus — Tiger Act

1. "Thunder and Blazes March"	Band forms circus ring
2. "Tiger Rag"	Drum Major and sousaphones do tiger act.
3. "Big Cage" March	Exit

Colonial — Show (America)

1. "Doxology"	Pilgrim Hat
2. "Minuet"	Date (1612)
3. "Yankee Doodle"	Liberty Bell

Compass (Geography) Show

1. "This Great Big Wonderful World"	Compass
2. "Sidewalks of New York"	Needle points east
3. "Baby, It's Cold Outside"	Needle points north
4. "Home on the Range"	Needle points west
5. "Are You from Dixie"	Needle points south

Coney Island

1. "By the Sea"	Boat or oldtime bathing suit style show
2. "While Strollin' thru the Park One Day"	Band step routine or Straw Hat Merry-Go-Round
3. "Yankee Doodle"	

Conference Show (for first game)

1. Play state song	State Outline
2. Fanfare and Home school Song	Majorettes locate conference schools on map
3. "Who"	Question Mark (for winner)

Cowboy Show

1. "Home on the Range"	Cabin
2. "Wagon Wheels"	Wheel

3. "I'm an Old Cowhand" — Cow Horns
4. "Deep in the Heart of Texas" — Star

Cuban Show
1. "Cuban Pete" — Band Rhumba or make Sombrero
2. "Copa Cabana" — Band Samba or make Palm Tree
3. "Querido Mambo" — Band Mambo or make Girl Figure
4. "Begin the Beguine" — Band Beguine or make Guitar

Dance Carnival
1. "Chicken Reel" — Square Dance or make Pitchfork
2. "Blue Danube" — Waltz or make Moon
3. "Old Dutch Garden" — Clog Dance or make Windmill
4. "Irish Washerwoman" — Reel or make Shamrock

Dances through the Years
1. Minuet — Make Dates
   "Minuet in G" — 1600
2. Square Dance
   "Turkey in the Straw" — 1700
3. Waltz
   "Blue Danube" — 1800
4. Charleston
   "Charleston" — 1900
5. Jitterbug or Rock
   "Rock around the Clock" — 1956

Day at the Zoo
1. "Tiger Rag" — Tiger
2. "Ferdinand the Bull" — Bull's Head
3. "Abba Dabba Honeymoon" — Monkey
4. "Old Dog Tray" — Dog
Note: Personnel in costumes can enter in cages

Democracy Show
1. "Dragnet" theme — Hammer and Sickle
2. "That's Where My Money Goes" — Dollar Sign (shrink it)
3. "Air Force Song" — Plane
4. "America the Beautiful" — Shield or Eagle

Depression Show
1. "Charleston" — 1928
2. "Pennies from Heaven" or "Sing a Song of Sixpence" — Dollar Sign
3. "Potatoes Are Cheaper" — Break $
4. "Keep Your Sunny Side Up" — Money Bag

Disneyland
1. "Mickey Mouse March" — Entrance
2. Frontierland
   "Ballad of Davy Crocket" — Hat and Gun
3. Tomorrowland
   "Stairway to the Stars" — Rocketship
4. Fantasyland
   "Heigh-Ho, Heigh-Ho or "Some Day My Prince Will Come" — Dwarf or Pick / Castle
5. Main Street
   "Trolley Song" — Trolley

Dixieland Show
1. "Way Down Yonder in New Orleans" — Clef Sign or Musical Notes
2. "Lassus Trombone" — Trombone
3. "Waitin' for the Robert E. Lee" — River Boat

Dragnet
1. "Dragnet" theme — Badge
2. "Who" — Mask
3. "All Pals Together" — Handcuffs
4. "I'm in the Jailhouse Now" — Jail
5. "Chain Gang" — Pick or Ball and Chain or band does drag step

Dutch Show
1. "In an Old Dutch Garden" — Windmill
2. "Tiptoe through the Tulips" — Tulip
3. "Netherlands Hymn" — Dutch Shoe

Election Show
1. "Who" — Question Mark
2. "Elephant Tango" — Elephant
3. "Donkey Serenade" — Donkey
4. "America" or "Stars and Stripes Forever" — Shield or "U.S.A."

Eskimo
1. "Baby, It's Cold Outside" — Igloo
2. "Cuddle up a Little Closer" — Thermometer

37

Famous Dance Bands

1. Harry James
   "Ciribiribin" — Trumpet
2. Glenn Miller
   "Moonlight Serenade" — Trombone
3. Benny Goodman
   "And the Angels Sing" — Clarinet
4. Exit (and Entrance)
   "There's No Business
   like Show Busines" — Block Band

Flapper Follies

1. "Charleston" — Band Dance or
   College
   Pennant
2. Any "Dixieland" tune — Jazz Band
3. "Bunny Hug" — Old Auto

Flower Show

1. "Send Her One Dozen Roses" — Rose or Box
2. "Apple Blossom Time" — Tree with
   paper prop
   blossoms
3. "When You Wore a Tulip" — Tulip (open it)
4. "Flowers for Madam" — Bouquet

Four Freedoms (UN)

1. Life
   "School Days" — Book
2. Liberty
   "Liberty Bell" — Statue of
   Liberty or
   Torch

3. Religion
   "Beautiful Savior" — Cross
4. Happiness
   "America" — "USA" or
   Shield

German Show

1. "Ach Du Lieber Augustine" — Beer Stein or
   Barrel
2. German Band Tune — Clown Band
3. "Vienna Woods" — Waltz Routine
4. "Under the Double Eagle" — Exit

Good Old Days

1. "Sidewalks of New York" — Entrance and
   Exit
2. "Only a Bird in a Gilded
   Cage" — Cage and
   Prop Bird
3. "Daisy, Daisy" — Bicycle
4. "Stein Song" — Beer Stein
5. "Trolley Song" — Trolley Car
6. "Take Me Out to the
   Ball Game" — Bat and Ball
7. "Meet Me in St. Louis" — Trumpet

Growing Up

1. "School Days" — School House
   or Book or
   Bell
2. "Graduation Day" — Diploma
3. "You Made Me Love You" — Heart
4. "Wedding March" — Church
5. "Rock-A-By-Baby" — Cradle or Baby
   Carriage

University of Michigan Marching Band, Ann Arbor, Michigan
William D. Revelli, Director. Shield Formation for "Four Freedoms" Band Show

Gypsy Show
1. "Play Gypsy" — Fiddle
2. "Slumber on My Little Gypsy Sweetheart" — Gypsy Cart or Tambourine
3. "Golden Earings" — Tent

Half Century of Hit Tunes
1. "The Bowery" — Derby and Cane
2. "In My Merry Oldsmobile" — Old Auto
3. "Swannee" — Kneeling Figure
4. "This Is the Army Mr. Jones" — Gun
5. Latest Pop Tune

Halloween
1. "Old Black Magic" or "It's Magic" — Witch or Broom
2. "Peter, Peter, Pumpkin Eater" — Jack-O-Lantern
3. "Shine on Harvest Moon" — Moon

Harvest Time
1. "Turkey in the Straw" — Corn Shocks
2. "We Gather Together" or "Doxology" — Cross
3. "Chicken Reel" — Square Dance

Hawaiian Show
1. "Hawaiian War Chant" — Palm Tree
2. "Song of the Islands" — Guitar
3. "Little Grass Shack" — Shack
4. "Aloha Oe" — Ship

Heart Theme
1. "My Heart Stood Still" — **Heart**
2. "With a Song in My Heart" — Musical note in heart
3. "Zing Went the Strings of My Heart" — Lyre in Heart
4. "Two Hearts Beat in ¾ Time" — Double Heart

Holiday Show
1. Armed Forces Day "You're in the Army Now" — Cannon
2. Thanksgiving "Turkey in the Straw" — Turkey
3. Christmas "White Christmas" — Tree
4. Valentine's Day "I Love You Truly" — Heart
5. Easter "Easter Parade" — Flower or Cross
6. Fourth of July "There'll Be a Hot Time in the Old Town Tonight" — Firecracker

Holidays
1. Happy Holidays" — Entrance
2. New Year's "Old Lang Syne" — Scythe
3. Valentine's Day "Let Me Call You Sweetheart" — Heart

University of Florida "Gator" Band, Gainesville, Florida
Harold Bachman, Director. Christmas Tree Formation for "Holiday" Band Show

4. Easter
   "Christ the Lord Is Risen Today" — Cross
5. Fourth of July
   "Yankee Doodle" — Firecracker or Rocket
6. Labor Day
   "Anvile Chorus" — Anvil or Wheel
7. Armed Forces Day
   "Something About a Soldier" — Gun
8. Thanksgiving
   "Over the River and through the Wods" — Turkey
9. Christmas
   "Silent Night" — Christmas Tree

Horse Act (for Circus)
1. "Go Galop" — Band in circle. Horses enter in pairs (Majorettes with plumes)
2. "Light Cavalry" (Allegro) — Galop
3. "Vienna Woods" — Waltz Act
4. Pop Song — Fox Trot

Houses around the World
1. "Japanese Sandman" — Pagoda
2. "Baby, It's Cold Outside" — Igloo
3. "Penthouse Serenade" — Skyscraper
4. "Indian Boy" — Tepee
5. "Home Sweet Home" or "This Old House" — House

Houses in America
1. "Home Sweet Home" — Entrance and Exit
2. "Shanty in Old Shanty Town" — Shanty
3. "Adobe Hacienda" — Alamo
4. "Little Grey Home in the West" — Cottage
5. "This Old House" — House (wreck it)

Hunting Show
1. "Hunting Scene" (Buchtel) — Dog
2. "William Tell" Allegro — Use Animated Gun and Lazy Dog comedy routine.
3. "Light Cavalry" Allegro —

Italian Show
1. "Funiculi Funicula" — Volcano
2. "Italian Street Song" — Guitar
3. "Gondolier's Song" — Gondola

Ice Show
1. "Winter Wonderland" — Prop snow flakes in large geometrical designs carried by Majorettes
2. "Skater's Waltz" — Band Glide-step routine
3. "Sleigh Ride" — Sleigh with streamers to Majorettes
4. "Jingle Bells" — Exit

Indian Show
1. "Indian Boy" (Bennett) — Entrance and Exit
2. "Indian Love Call" — Canoe
3. "Land of the Sky Blue Water" — Wigwam

Irish Show
1. "Irish Washerwoman" — Entrance
2. "Come Back to Erin" — Shamrock
3. "When Irish Eyes Are Smiling" — Face and Prop Eyes
4. "The Harp That Once through Tara's Hall" — Harp

Jungle Show
1. "Voodoo" (Walters) — Tom-tom or Cooking Pot
2. "Jungle Jump" (Handlon) — Dance Routine or Jungle House
3. "If I'd Known You Were A-Comin' " — Safari Rescue Act

Kiddieland
1. "Here We Go round the Mulberry Bush" — Spiral
2. "London Bridge Is Fallin' Down" — Bridge (collapse it)
3. "See Saw Marjorie Daw" — See-Saw
4. "Twinkle, Twinkle, Little Star" — Star

Last Home Game
1. School Song — School Letter or School House
2. "School Days" — Recognize Team or Seniors in Band
3. "Pomp and Circumstance" — Exit

Life of a Working Girls (School Teacher)

1. "Rise and Shine"   Alarm Clock
2. "Trolley Song" or   Trolley or Car
   "Merry Oldsmobile"
3. "School Days"   Desk or School
                                    House
4. "Sleepy Time Gal"   Rocking Chair

Little Red Riding Hood

1. "Oh You Beautiful Doll"   Doll or
                                   Stick Figure
2. "A Tisket, A Tasket"   Basket
3. Spook Music   Wolf Head or
                                   Stick Figure
4. "This Old House"   House
5. "Who's Afraid of the Big   Stick Wolf
   Bad Wolf"   (chop head
                                   with prop
                                   ax)

Use Narrator to tell story.

Mardi Gras

1. "Way Down Yonder in New   Cotton Bale
   Orleans"
2. "Waiting for the Robert   River Boat
   E. Lee"
3. "Can-Can" (Orpheus)   Dance Routine
4. "Deep River"   River
5. "Saints Come Marchin' In"   Trumpet

Mexican Fiesta

1. "Down Mexico Way" or   Map or Plane
   "South of the Border"
2. "Chiapenecas"   Clap Hands
                                   Routine
3. "Jarabe Tapetio"   Sombrero
   (Mexican Hat Dance)
4. "La Golondrina" or   Guitar
   "Estrellita"
5. "Zacatecas"   Exit

Moon Show

1. "Shine on Harvest Moon"   Full Moon
2. "Only a Paper Moon"   Half Moon and
                                   a Star
3. "Moon over Miami"   Moon and
                                   Palm Tree
4. "Blue Moon"   Use Cap Lights
5. "By the Light of the   Exit
   Silvery Moon"

Mule Show (Political)

1. "On the Trail"   Ears
2. "Old Grey Mare"   Novelty March-
                                   ing Routine
3. "Donkey Serenade"   Musical Note
4. "I Get a Kick Out of You"   Animated
                                   Stick Mule

University of Michigan Marching Band, Ann Arbor, Michigan
William D. Revelli, Director.   Block "M" Formation for "Last Home Game" Show

41

Musical Instrument Show

1. "Say It with Music"	Entrance and Exit
2. "Ring, Ring De Banjo"	Banjo
3. "Ciribiribin"	Cornet
4. "Clarinet Polka"	Clarinet
5. "Lassus Trombone"	Trombone
6. "Piccolo Pete"	Flute or Rhumba Routine
7. "When Yuba Plays the Tuba"	Bass Horn

Nautical Show

1. "By the Sea"	Entrance
2. "Shipmates Forever"	Boat
3. "Bell Bottom Trousers"	Majorette Dance
4. "Anchors Aweigh"	Anchor
5. "Sailing, Sailing"	Exit

Oklahoma

1. "Oh, What a Beautiful Morning"	Sun
2. "Surrey with the Fringe on Top"	Surrey
3. "People Will Say We're in Love"	Heart
4. "Oklahoma"	Map
5. "Kansas City"	Exit

Old Man River

1. "Waiting for the Robert E. Lee"	Steam Boat
2. "Old Man River"	Banjo or Cotton Bale
3. "Mardi Gras"	Crown
4. "Hear that Dixieland Band"	Circle with Dixieland Band in center

Old Soldiers Never Die

1. "Yankee Doodle"	Musket or "76"
2. "We're Tenting Tonight on the Old Campground"	Tent
3. "When Johnny Comes Marching Home"	Spanish-American War Date
4. "Over There"	Cannon
5. "Praise the Lord and Pass the Ammunition"	Plane
6. "Red, White, and Blue"	Exit

Parade of Girls

1. "Margie"	Flapper
2. "Betty Co-ed"	College Girl
3. "Marie"	Hometown Girl
4. "Valencia" or "Rosalie"	Spanish Girl
5. "Dinah"	Southern Belle
6. "Mary"	Old-Fashioned Girl

Use Narrator and girls in costumes

Plantation Days

1. "Dixie"	Entrance and Confederate Flag
2. "Old Folks At Home"	Steamboat
3. "Old Man River"	Cotton Bale
4. "Are You from Dixie?"	Dixie and Exit

Prohibition

1. "Little Brown Jug"	Jug
2. "How Dry I Am"	Lamppost
3. "Pepsi Cola Song"	School Letter

Railroad Show

1. "Casey Jones" or "She'll Be Comin' round the Mountain"	Entrance
2. "Down by the Station"	Majorette Routine with lanterns
3. "Chattanooga Choo-Choo"	Locomotive
4. "I've Been Working on the Railroad"	Exit

Round-Up Time

1. "Round-up Time in Texas"	Entrance
2. "I'm an Old Cowhand"	Saddle
3. "Home on the Range"	Tent or Cactus
4. "Git Along Little Dogie"	Cow Horns
5. "Deep in the Heart of Texas"	Exit

Rose Marie Show

1. "Totem Tom Tom"	Totem Pole or Drum
2. "Rose Marie"	Solo (vocal)
3. "Indian Love Call"	Wigwam or Canoe

Safety Education (Road Signs)

1. "Little Red Caboose" or "Railroad Song"	R.R. Crossing Sign
2. "Beware My Foolish Heart"	Caution Sign
3. "Stop, You're Breaking My Heart"	Stop Sign

Sailor Ashore
1. "Bell Bottom Trousers" — Entrance
2. "Sailing, Sailing" — Ship
3. "Sailor's Hornpipe" — Dance
4. "Hawaiian War Chant" — Ukelele
5. "Anchors Aweigh" — Exit

St. Patrick's Day
1. "Great Day for the Irish" — Entrance or Shamrock
2. "Irish Washerwoman" — Majorette Dance
3. "When Irish Eyes Are Smiling" — Solo Irish Harp
4. "Come Back to Erin"

Salute To The Flag
1. "American Patrol" — Entrance or USA
2. "Yankee Doodle" — Spirit of '76 Act
3. "It's a Grand Old Flag" — Flag
4. "Stars and Stripes Forever" — Exit

Scenes from Operaland
1. "Anvil Chorus" — Anvil
2. "Faust Waltz" — Sword or Dance
3. "Toreador Song" — Bullfight or Matador's hat
4. "William Tell" — Apple or Bow and Arrow

Note: Use "Scenes from Operaland" H. Fillmore, Pub. C. Fischer

Seasons
1. Spring
   "April Showers" or "June Is Bustin' Out All Over" — Flower or Heart
2. Summer
   "Yankee Doodle" or "Lazy Bones" — Firecracker or Fishing Rod
3. Fall
   "Harvest Moon" or "Autumn Leaves" — Moon or Leaf
4. Winter
   "Winter Wonderland" or "Auld Lang Syne" — Christmas Tree

Shoe Show
1. "Oh Dem Golden Slippers" — Slipper
2. "I Got Shoes" — Shoe with Wings
3. "Blue Suede Shoes" — Dance Routine

4. "In an Old Dutch Garden" — Dutch Clog
5. "I Got Spurs" — Western Boot
6. "Chattanooga Shoe-Shine Boy" — Boot

Showboat
1. "Captain Andy" — Entrance
2. "Old Man River" — Cotton Bale
3. "Only Make Believe" — Broken Heart
4. "Showboat" — Animated Showboat

Sidewalks of New York
1. "East Side, West Side" — Skyscraper
2. "Bicycle Built for Two" — Bike
3. "While Strolling through the Park One Day" — Derby and Cane
4. "Take Me Out to the Ball Game" — Bat and Ball
5. "Casey Danced with the Strawberry Blond" — Band Dance

Sky Show
1. "Stardust" or "Twinkle, Twinkle Little Star" — Star
2. "When the Moon Comes Over the Mountain" — Moon and Mountain
3. "Lucky Old Sun" — Sun with Rays

South-American Show
1. "Brazil" — Coffee Bag
2. "Down Mexico Way" — Volcano
3. "Chiquita Banana" — Banana
4. "Managua Nicaragua" — Map
5. "El Rancho Rio Grande" — Guitar
6. "South American Way" — Exit

South Pacific Show
1. "Bali Hai" — Palm Tree
2. "I'm Goin' to Wash That Man Right Out of my Hair" — Sailor
3. "Some Enchanted Evening" — Moon
4. "Younger than Springtime" — Heart

Space Cadet Show
1. "Stairway to the Stars" — Stairway
2. "Blue Moon" — Moon
3. "Stardust" — Star
4. "Mars at Midnight" — Space Ship

Spanish Show
1. "Toreador Song" — Matador's Hat
2. "Lady in Red" — Fan
3. "Valencia" — Guitar
4. "Ferdinand the Bull" — Bull Fight

Sports Review
1. Fooball — Goal Post
   "Betty Co-ed"
2. Baseball
   "Take Me Out to the — Ball and Bat
   Ball Game"
3. Basketball — School Letter
   School Pep Song
4. Track — Winged Shoe
   "The Man on the
   Flying Trapeze"
5. Swimming — Beach and
   "Over the Waves" — umbrella

States, Parade of
1. "Dixie" — Entrance
2. Louisiana — Map
   "Louisiana Hayride"
3. North Carolina — Map
   "Carolina Moon"
4. South Carolina — Map
   "Carolina in the
   Morning" — Map

5. Mississippi
   "Waiting for the — Map
   Robert E. Lee"
6. Georgia
   "Sweet Georgia Brown — Map
   or "Georgia Camp
   Meeting
7. Kentucky — Map
   "Old Kentucky Home"
8. Tennessee — Map
   "Tennessee Waltz"
9. Missouri — Map
   "Missouri Waltz"
10. Arkansas — Map
    "Arkansas Traveler"
11. Ohio — Map
    "Down By the O-Hi-O"
12. Indiana — Map
    "Back Home Again in
    Indiana"
13. Texas — Map
    "Eyes of Texas"
14. California — Map

University of Florida "Gator" Band, Gainesville, Florida
Harold Bachman, Director. Outline of the State of Louisiana Formation

"California, Here I
  Come"
15. Wyoming   Map
    "Roaming in Wyoming"
16. Pennsylvania   Map
    "Pennsylvania Polka"
17. New York   Map
    "Sidewalks of New
      York"
18. Virginia   Map
    "Trail of the Lonesome
      Pine"
19. Oklahoma   Map
    "Oklahoma"
20. Alabama   Map
    "Stars Fell on
      Alabama"
    "Alabamy Bound"
21. Florida
    "Moon Over Miami"
Note: Select from list to build
    show.

State Fair
1. "Meet Me in St. Louis,   Ferris Wheel
   Louie"
2. "I'm Forever Blowing   Balloon and
   Bubbles"   String
3. "The Merry-Go-Round   Carousel
   Broke Down"
4. "Wheel of Fortune"   Wheel
5. "Hawaiian War Chant" Side Show
6. "Oh, You Beautiful Doll" Doll
7. "There'll Be a Hot Time in Exit
   the Old Town Tonight"

Storm Show
1. "Stormy Weather"   Entrance and
                  Cloud
2. "Umbrella Song"   Umbrella
                  (open and
                  close it)
3. "I'm Singing in the Rain" Majorette
                  routine with
                  umbrellas
4. "Somewhere over the   Rainbow
   Rainbow"   Exit
5. "Look for the Silver Lining"

Swim Time
1. "By the Sea"   Umbrella and
                  beach girl in
                  Gay 90's
                  swim suit
2. "Charleston"   Girl in 1920
                  swim suit

3. "Lady in Red"   Girl in one-
                  piece red
                  suit
4. "A Pretty Girl Is Like a Girl in Bikini
   Melody"
5. "Dungaree Doll"   Comedy Sketch

Style Show through the Years
1. "Yankee Doodle"   Costumed
                  Colonial Girl
                  or "Blunder-
                  buss" for-
                  mation
2. "Davy Crockett"   Pioneer Girl
                  or Ax forma-
                  tion
3. "Alabamy Bound"   Hoop-skirted
                  Girl or Cabin
                  formation
4. "A Pretty Girl Is like a Gay 90's Girl
   Melody"   or Bicycle
                  formation
5. "Charleston"   Flapper Girl
                  or Old Auto
                  formation
6. Latest Pop Tune   Bathing Girl
                  or Rocket
                  formation

Three Ring Circus
1. "Thunder and Blazes   3 Rings or
   March"   Tent
2. "Tiger Rag"   Cat Act Center
                  Ring
3. "Light Cavalry"   Horse Act-Left
                  Ring
4. "Go Galop"   Tumblers-Right
                  Ring
5. "Show Boy March"   Finale in 3
                  Rings and
                  Exit

Time Marches On
1. "Rock-A-By-Baby"   Cradle
2. "London Bridge"   Bridge
3. "School Days"   School House
4. "Betty Co-ed"   Pennant
5. "Wedding March"   Church
6. "Rock-A-By-Baby"   Exit

Time Show
1. "Syncopated Clock"   Clock
2. "As Time Goes By"   Hour Glass
3. "Now Is the Hour"   Watch
4. "Time on My Hands" Wrist Watch
5. "It's Later than You Think" Exit

Toy Store Show

1. "Parade of the Wooden Soldiers" — Entrance
2. "Lone Ranger Theme" (Wm. Tell) — Rocking Horse
3. "Hawaiian War Chant" — Ukelele
4. "March of the Toys" — Soldie Doll
5. "Chattanooga Choo-Choo" — Train
6. "Oh, You Beautiful Doll" — Doll

Transportation Show

1. "Horses, Horses" — Entrance or Saddle
2. "Wagon Wheels" — Wagon
3. "In My Merry Oldsmobile" — Auto
4. "Air Corps Song" — Plane
5. "Mars at Midnight" — Rocket

Tribute to School Staff

1. "School Days" — Entrance and Exit
2. Principal — Mortarboard Hat
   "For He's a Jolly Good Fellow"
3. Teacher — Apple (use prop worm for gag)
   "An Apple for the Teacher"
4. Janitor — Broom
   "Whistle While You Work"
5. Cafeteria — Knife-Fork
   "Shortnin' Bread"
6. Coaches — Clover
   I'm Looking Over a Four Leaf Clover"
7. School — Monogram
   School Song

Touring Europe

1. "Over the Waves" — Boat
2. "London Bridge" or Pomp and Circumstance" — Bridge or Crown
3. "In an Old Dutch Garden" — Windmill
4. "Can-Can" — Eiffel Tower
5. "Ach Du Lieber Augustine" — Beer Stein
6. "Ferdinand the Bull" — Bull, Ring, and Fight

T-V Ads

1. "Chevy Song" — T-V-Set
2. "Dragnet" Theme — Badge or Gun
3. "Land of the Sky Blue Waters" — Beer Stein
4. "Smoke Gets in Your Eyes" or "Lucky Strike" theme — Cigarette
5. "Look Sharp March" — Safety Razor
6. "In My Merry Oldsmobile" — Auto

T-V Comedians

1. Bob Hope
   "Thanks for the Memories" — Ski Slide
2. Jimmy Durante
   "Diga,Diga,Doo" — Nose
3. Jack Benny
   "Hearts and Flowers" — Fiddle
4. Eddie Cantor
   "If You Knew Susie" — Hands or Eyes

United Nations

1. "America the Beautiful" — Entrance and Parade of Flags
2. "La Marseillaise" — Eiffel Tower
3. "Volga Boatman" — Anvil
4. "Pomp and Circumstance" — Crown
5. "American Patrol"
6. "Stars and Stripes Forever" — "U.N."

United States Salute

1. "American Exultant March" — Entrance
2. "Broadway Melody — Skyscraper
3. "Chicago" — Elevated Train
4. "Missouri Waltz" — Mule
5. "Stars Fell in Alabama" — Star
6. "California Here I Come" — Sun
7. "It's a Grand Old Flag" — Flag

U.S. History Show

1. "Indian Boy March" — Tepee
2. "Doxology" — Pilgrim Hat
3. "Yankee Doodle" — Firecracker
4. "Dixie" — Parade Confederate and U.S. Flags
5. "Over There" — Cannon
6. "Remember Pearl Harbor or "Praise the Lord and Pass the Ammunition" — Ship or Plane
7. "America the Beautiful" — "USA"

Vacationland, U.S.A.

1. "By the Sea" — Beach and Umbrella
2. "Lazy Bones" — Fishing Rod
3. "Turkey in the Straw" — Dance Routine
4. "When the Moon Comes Over the Mountain" or "On Top of Old Smoky" — Mountain
5. "Sailing, Sailing" — Sail Boat
6. "Highways Are Happy Ways" — Auto

Vacation Show
1. "Sailing, Sailing" — Boat
2. "Stars of the Summer Night" — Star
3. "Lazy Bones" — Fishing Rod
4. "Ragtime Cowboy Joe" — Cowboy Hat
5. "In My Merry Oldsmobile" — Car

Valentine Day
1. "Let Me Call You Sweetheart" — Heart andArrow
2. "A Pretty Girl Is like a Melody" — Majorettes in Style Show
3. "I Love You a Bushel and a Peck" — Basket
4. "Mother Macree" — Rocking Chair

Weather Show
1. "Stormy Weather" — Entrance
2. "Let a Smile Be Your Umbrella" — Umbrella

3. "Button Up Your Overcoat" — Overcoat
4. "April Showers" — Flower
5. "Look for the Silver Lining" — Rainbow
6. "Blue Skies" — Sunburst

World Tour
1. "Maple Leaf Forever" or "Oh Canada" — Maple Leaf
2. "Rule Brittania" (England) — Crown
3. "Can-Can" (France) — Eiffel Tower
4. "Chiapenecas" (Mexico) — Sombrero
5. "La Golondrina" (Spain) — Fan
6. "Funiculi Funicula" (Italy) — Gondola
7. "Chinese Temple Garden" — Pagoda

Westward Ho
1. 'Wagon Wheels" — Wagon
2. "Home on the Range" — Campfire Scene
3. "Indian Boy" — Indian Attack
4. "California Here I Come" — Exit

University of Oregon Marching Band, Eugene, Oregon
Robert Vagner, Director. Covered Wagon Formation for "Westward Ho" Band Show

47

CHAPTER IV

906 WELL - KNOWN TUNES WITH SHOW IDEAS

The composer, arranger, and publisher are given as far as possible. Some tunes are published in several arrangements by different publishers.

Most music stores or jobbers can supply a director with any tune published for band provided the title is given.

"Ach Du Lieber Augustine"
("Where Oh Where")
   Traditional — Dog's Head
   Pub. Ascher — Wiener
     Dog

"Across the Field"
   (Ohio State) — Football
   Pub. Morris — Helmet
     Goalpost
     Football

"Across the Wide Missouri"
   Arr. Walters — Book — River
   Pub. Rubank — State Outline
     Covered Wagon

"Adeste Fidelis"
   Reading — Cross
   Pub. Belwin — Christmas Tree
     Briegel — Christmas
     Kjos — Wreath
     G. Schirmer — Candle

"After Graduation Day"
   S. Lippman — Graduation Cap
   Pub. Chappell — Tied Diploma
     '58, '59, etc.

"After the Ball"
   Pub. Rubank — Gay 90's Skit
     Carl Fischer — Hat and Cane
     Tandem Bike

"A Guy Is a Guy"
   Arr. Leonard — Drill Routine
   Pub. Leonard — Crewcut Head
     Stick Man

"Ah, Sweet Mystery of Life"
   Herbert
   Arr. Teague — Fiddle
   Pub. MPH — Question Mark

"Ain't She Sweet"
   Ager — Girl's Head
   Pub. MPH — Stick Woman

"Ain't We Got Fun"
   Kahn-Egan-Whiting — Banjo
   Arr. Teague — School House
   Pub. MPH — Sun and Moon

"Air Force Song"
   Crawford — Plane
   Pub. Carl Fischer — Parachute
     Jet Plane
     Shield

"Alabamy Bound"
   DeSylva-Green-Henderson — Cotton Bale
   Pub. Shapiro — Locomotive
     State Map

"Alexander's Ragtime Band"
   I. Berlin — Combo Band
   Arr. Yoder — Note
   Pub. Berlin — Trumpet

"Alice Blue Gown"
   McCarthy-Tierney — Girl
   Arr. Beeler
   Pub. Big 3

"All Alone by the Telephone"
(Octavo)
   Pub. Berlin — Telephone

"All-American Girl"
"Feist Football Medley"
   Pub. Big 3 — Football
     Girl
     Goalpost

"All I Want for Christmas Is My Two Front Teeth"
   Pub. MPH — Face and Teeth
     Christmas Tree

"All My Love"
   Arr. Schoenfeld — Heart
   Pub. MPH

"All of Me"
   Simons — Stick Figure
   Arr. Hill — (Take Away
   Pub. Bourne — Parts)

"All, or Nothing at All"*
   Altman — Microphone
     Bow Tie

---

*Not published in band arrangement; available in piano, vocal, or dance orchestra arrangements.

"Almost Like Being in Love"
Lerner
Pub. Fox   Heart

"Aloha Oe"
Liliuokalani
Pub. Hansen - Book   Finale Tune
Also American Collection-Book   Guitar
Pub. Rubank   Palm Tree
Carl Fischer   Boat

"Amapola"
Lacalle
Arr. Beeler   Fan
Pub Marks   Gutar

"America"
Traditional   Capitol
Arr. Fillmore   Flag
Pub. Associated   Military Cap
Barnhouse   Shield
Briegel   Statue of
Carl Fischer   Liberty
Rubank   USA
Volkwein   Torch

"America, I Love You"
Arr. Lang   Flag
Pub. Mills   Shield
       "USA" in heart

"America the Beautiful"
Traditional   Capitol
Pub. Associated   Flag
Briegel   Statue of
Carl Fischer   Liberty
Kjos   Shield
Rubank   "USA"
       Torch
       Military Cap

"American Patrol"
Meacham   Flag
Pub. Ascher   Capitol
Associated   Military Hat
Belwin   Statue of
Kjos   Liberty
Rubank   Shield
       Torch
       "USA"

"April in Paris"
V. Duke   Calendar
Pub. MPH   Eiffel Tower

"April Showers"
Silvers   Clouds
Arr. Teague   Flowers
Pub. MPH   Rainbow
       Umbrella
       Watering Can

"An Apple for the Teacher"
Monaco
Arr. Briegel   School House
Pub. Joy   Apple

"Anchor's Aweigh"
Arr. Yoder   Anchor
Pub. Big 3   Ship
       Sailboat
       Shield - "N"

"Anniversary Song"
Jolson   Cake
Arr. Choplin   Figures "50,"
Pub. Shapiro   "75," etc.
       Hearts
       entwined
       Rings
       interlocked

"Anniversary Waltz"
Dabin   Cake
Arr. Franklin   Figures "60,"
Pub. Morris   "75," etc.
       Rings
       Interlocked
       Hearts
       entwined

"Anvil Chorus"
Verdi   Horseshoe
Pub. Kjos   Anvil
Ludwig   Hammer

"Any Time"
Arr. Leonard   Clock
Pub. Leonard   Watch
       Hourglass

"A Perfect Day"
Bond
Pub. Boston   Sun (setting)

"A Pretty Girl Is like a Melody" (Octavo)
I. Berlin   Clef
Arr. Yoder   Heart
Pub. Berlin   Note
       Picture Frame

"Apple Blossom Time"
Arr. Leonard   Flower
Pub. Leonard   Tree

"April Blossoms"
Stothart-Youmans   Calendar
       Flower

"April In Paris"*
V. Duke   Eiffel Tower
       Lilac Blossom

"April in Portugal"
Pub. Chappell   Fan
       Calendar

"April Showers" (Octavo)
Silvers   Clouds and Rain
Arr. Teague   Flower
Pub. MPH   Rain

"Are You from Dixie"
Cobb   Banjo
Arr. Teague   Cotton Bale
Pub. MPH   River Boat

"Are You Sleeping"
Traditional
Arr. Walters — Alarm Clock
Pub. Rubank — Question Mark

"Arkansas Traveler"
Traditional — Barn
Pub. Belwin — Chicken
  Carl Fischer — Hog
  Haystack
  Mule
  Pitchfork
  State

"Asleep in the Deep"
Pub. MPH — Submarine

"As Time Goes By"
Hapfield
Arr. Schoenfield — Clock
Pub. MPH — Hour Glass

"At Dawning"
Cadman
Pub. Presser — Sun (rising)

"A Tisket, a Tasket, a Brown and Yellow Basket"
Feldman
Arr. Yoder
Pub. Big 3 — Basket

"At the Rodeo"
Van Alstyne — Boot
Arr. Schoenfield — Cowboy Hat
Pub MPH — Horse

"Auf Wiedersehen Sweetheart"
Arr. Leonard — Dance Routine
Pub. Leonard — Heart

"Auld Lang Syne"
Traditional
Pub. Belwin
  Briegel
  Hansen
  King
  Kjos — Finale Tune
  Leonard — Hour Glass
  Rubank — Year Numerals

"Autumn Nocturne" (Octavo)
Myrow
Arr. Teague — Calendar
Pub. MPH — Leaf

"Autumn Leaves"
Mercer — Tree
Pub. Hansen — Leaf

"Autumn Serenade" (Quarto)
P. DeRose — Leaf
Pub. Big 3 — Note

" 'A' You're Adorable"
Kaye-Wise-Lippman — Girl's Face
Pub. Leonard — Use Alphabet Cards

"Away in a Manger"
Traditional — Cross
Pub. Kjos — Candle
  Manger
  Christmas Wreath
  Christmas Tree
  Star

"Babes In Toyland" (Octavo)
V. Herbert — Candy Cane
Pub. MPH — Doll
  Toy Trumpet

"Baby Face"
Davis
Arr. Schoenfeld — Baby Carriage
Pub. MPH — Face

"Baby, It's Cold Outside"
Pub. Morris — Icicle
  Overcoat
  Thermometer

"Baby, Won't You Please Come Home"
Williams — House
Arr. Yoder — Moon
Pub. Leeds — Question Mark

"Back Home in Indiana"
Hanley — Barn
Pub. Shapiro — Cornstalk
  Hog
  Hay Wagon
  State

"Back in the Saddle Again"*
  Cowboy Hat
  Cowboy Boot
  Stick Horse
  Spurs

"Bali Hai"
Rodgers
Arr. Schoenfeld — Palm Tree
Pub. Chappell — Moon

"Ballin' the Jack"
Arr. Croy
Pub. Marks — Dance Routine

"Band Played On"
Ward
Pub. Ascher — Musical Instrument
  Leeds
  Rubank — Stage

"Barcarolle"
Offenbach
Pub. Carl Fischer — Gondola
  Rubank — Guitar

"Basin Street Blues"
S. Williams — Clarinet
Arr. Briegel — Cornet
Pub. Morris — Note

50

"Beal Street Blues"
W. C. Handy — Cornet
Pub. Handy — Clarinet
— Cotton Bale
— Note

"Bear Went over the Mountain"
Folk Tune — Bear
Pub. Belwin — Mountain

"Beat Of My Heart"*
— Heart (beating)

"Beautiful Brown Eyes"
Smith-Delmore
Arr. Herfurth — Eyes
Pub. Hansen — Spectacles

"Beautiful Colorado" (Octavo)
Pub. Carl Fischer — Mountains
— State Outline

"Beautiful Ohio"
McDonald-Earl
Arr. Briegel — State outline
Pub. Shapiro — "Ohio"

"Be Careful, It's My Heart"*
Berlin — Broken Heart

"Because of You"
Pub. Leonard — Stunt
— Juke Box

"Beer Barrel Polka" (Here Comes the Navy)
Vejroda — Barrel
Pub. Shapiro — Anchor

"Begin the Beguine"
C. Porter
Arr. Teague
Pub. MPH — Maracas

"Bell Bottom Trousers"*
Jaffe — Sailor Hat
Arr. Briegel — Ship
— Shield - "N"

"Bells of St. Mary's"
Adams
Arr. Yoder
Pub. Chappell — Bell

"Be Still, My Heart" *
— Heart

"Best Things in Life Are Free"
Pub. Chappell — Moon
— Tree
— Star
— Sun

"Betty Co-ed"
Vallee — Football
Arr. Brockton — Goalpost
Pub. Carl Fischer — Megaphone

"Beyond the Blue Horizon"
Robin
Arr. Whiting — Ship
Pub. Famous — Mountains

"Bicycle Built for Two"
Dacre
Pub. Ascher
Kjos — Bicycle
Leeds — Derby and Cane

"Bidin' My Time" (Octavo)
Gershwin — Clock
Arr. Schoenfeld — Sundial
Pub. MPH — Hour Glass

"Big Apple"*
— Apple
— Dance Routine

"Big Bass Viol"
Bohannon
Arr. Yoder
Pub. Rubank — Bass Fiddle

"Big Joe, the Tuba"
Lavalle
Pub. Fox — Tuba

"Big Rock Candy Mountain"
Folk Song
Pub. Ascher — Candy Cane
Rubank — Mountain

"Bim Bam Bum" (Rhumba)
Morales — Maracas
Pub. Big 3 — Sombrero

"Birth of the Blues" (Octavo)
Henderson — Cornet
Arr. Teague — Clarinet
Pub. MPH — Cotton Bale
— Note

"Blacksmith Blues"*
— Anvil
— Hammer

"Blow, Gabriel Blow" (Octavo)
C. Porter
Arr. Teague
Pub. MPH — Trumpet

"Blow the Man Down"
Traditional sailors song
Americana Collection-Book — Anchor
Pub. Rubank — Ship

"Blowin' the Blues Medley"
Arr. Yoder — Trumpet
Pub. Big 3 — Note

"Blue Bird of Happiness"*
S. Harmati — Bird
— (cap lights in blue)
— Lyre

"Blue Danube"
Strauss
Pub. Ascher
Carl Fischer — Castle
Rubank — River
Volkwein — Violin

51

"Blue Hawaii"
Robin — Boat
Pub. Famous — Palm Tree
— Palm Hut

"Blue Moon"
Rodgers
Arr. Bennett
Pub. Big 3 — Moon

"Blues in the Night"
H. Arlen
Arr. Teague — Note and Moon
Pub. MPH — Note and Star

"Blues On Parade"*
— Note
— Clef
— Staff

"Blue Skies"
I. Berlin
Arr. Yoder
Pub. Berlin — Clouds

"Blue Skirt Waltz"
Lang
Pub. Mills — Girl

"Blue Tango" (Quarto)
Anderson — Dance Routine
Pub. Mills — Guitar
— Spanish Fan

"Bonapart's Retreat"
Pub. Leonard — Drill Routine

"Boola-Boola" (Yale)
Arr. Leidzen — Bulldog
Pub. Big 3 — Football
— Helmet
— Goalposts

"Boots and Saddles"
Pub. Leonard — Boot
— Saddle
— Marching
— Routine

"Botch-A-Me"
Pub. Leonard — Drill Routine

"Bowery"
Percy Gaunt
Pub. Ascher
Kjos — Derby
Leeds — Cane

"Brazil" (Samba, Quarto)
Barroso
Arr. Smith — Maracas
Pub. Southern, N.Y. — Map of Brazil

"Brazilian National Hymn"
Pub. Kjos-Book — Country Outline
— Coffee Bag

"Broadway Melody"*
N. H. Brown — Note
— Staff
— Skyscraper
— Top Hat

"Brother Can You Spare A Dime"*
Gorney — Feather (red)
— Money
— Question Mark
— Red Cross

"Buckle Down Winsocki"
Martin-Blane
Arr. Schoenfeld — Football
Pub. Chappell — Goalpost

"Buffalo Gal, Won't Cha Come Out Tonight"
White
Pub. Ascher
Kjos — Dance Routine

"Bugle Call Rag"
Pettis-Meyers-Schoebel
Arr. Redfield
Pub. Mills — Bugle

"Bunny Hop"
Pub. Leonard — Dance Routine
— Rabbit

"Bury Me Not on the Lone Prairie"
Cowboy Song
Pub. Belwin-Book
Hansen-Book — Cowboy Hat
Kjos — Tombstone

"Bushel and A Peck"
Loesser — Big Heart and
Pub. Frank — Small Heart
— Basket

"Button Up Your Overcoat"
DeSylva — Igloo
Pub. Chappell — Icicle
— Thermometer

"Buttons and Bows"
Livingston-Evans — Bow and
Pub. Famous — Buttons

"Bye-Bye-Blackbird"
Henderson
Arr. Schoenfeld
Pub. MPH — Bird

"Bye Bye Blues"
Hamm-Bennett-Lown-Gray — Note
Pub. Bourne-Book — Clef
— Staff

"By the Light of the Silvery Moon"
Edwards — Canoe
Arr. Teague — Boat
Pub. MPH — Moon

"By the Sea, By the Beautiful Sea"
Arr. Yoder or Bennett — Beach and
Pub. Shapiro — Umbrella
— Sail Boat

"By the Waters of the Minnetonka" (Octavo)
Malnek — Indian Head
Pub. Presser — Canoe

"Cabin in the Sky"*
V. Duke — Cabin and Moon

"Caisson Song" (U.S. Field Artillery)
Gruber
Pub. Ascher
Associated
Big 3
Carl Fischer
Kjos
Shapiro — Cannon

"California Here I Come"
Jolson
Arr. Lindeman — Covered Wagon
Pub. MPH — State

"Camptown Races"
Foster — Horse
Pub. Carl Fischer — Minstrel Man
Kjos — Tambourine

"Canadian Capers" (Octavo)
Chandler
Arr. Teague — Ice Skate
Pub. MPH — Maple Leaf

"Can Anyone Explain"
Leonard
Pub. Leonard — Question Mark

"Can-Can"
Offenbach
Pub. Hansen-Book — Eiffel Tower
Kjos — Dance Routine

"Can't Get Indiana Off My Mind"
Carmichael
Arr. Briegel — State Outline
Pub. Mills — Tractor

"Can This Be Love"*
K. Swift — Heart and Question Mark

"Can't You Hear Me Callin' Caroline"
Roma — Map - N.C.
Arr. Teague — Map - S.C.
Pub. MPH — Megaphone
Telephone

"Carolina in the Morning"
W. Donaldson — Locomotive
Arr. Teague — State Outline
Pub. MPH — Sun (rising)

"Carolina Moon" (Octavo)
Arr. Yoder — Moon
Pub. Morris — Mountain
State Outline

"Casey Jones"
Newton
Arr. Yoder — Engineer's Hat
Pub. Shapiro — Locomotive

"Cement Mixer Song"*
Cement Mixer

"Charleston"
Mack-Johnson
Arr. Schoenfeld — Dance Routine
Pub. MPH — Old Auto

"Charlie Is My Darlin' "
Pub. Rubank-Book — Cane
Derby Hat
Eyes

"Charmaine"
Pollack
Arr. Yoder — Eiffel Tower
Pub. Big 3 — Girl

"Chattanooga Choo Choo"
Warren-Gordon
Arr. Yoder — Locomotive
Pub. Big 3 — Engineer's Hat

"Chattanooga Shoe Shine Boy"
Stone
Arr. Leonard
Pub. Leonard
Also
Arr. Herfurth
Pub. Hansen — Shoe

"Cherokee"
Noble — Tomahawk
Pub. Shapiro — Tepee

"Chevy Song"*
Auto

"See the U.S.A. in Your Chevolet"
Carr
Arr. Schoenfeld
Pub. Chappell

"Chiapenecas" (Clap Hands)
Campo
Pub. Kjos — Donkey
Leonard — Sombrero
Marks — Volcano

"Chicago"
Fisher — Elevated Train
Pub. Hansen — Skyscraper

"Chicken Reel"
Traditional — Barn
Pub. Big 3 — Dance Routine
Carl Fischer — Egg (break it)
Hay Stack
Pitchfork

"Chimes of Spring"
Lincke — Flower
Pub. Marks — Bell
Calendar

53

"China Boy"
Winfree
Arr. Yoder	Pagoda
Pub. Big 3	Rickshaw

"China Town"
Schwartz
Arr. Teague	Pagoda
Pub. MPH	Rickshaw

"Cielito Lindo"
Fernandez
Pub. Ascher	Guitar

"Cindy"
Pub. Marks	Girl

"Ciribiribin"
Pestolozza
Pub. Ascher
Carl Fischer
Kjos	Trumpet
Rubank	Gondola

"Clang, Clang, Clang, Went the Trolley"
Pub. Big 3	Trolley Car

"Clap Hands" (Chiapenecas)
De Campo
Pub. Kjos
Leonard	Sombrero
Marks	Volcano

"Clap Yo' Hands" (Octavo)
Gershwin	Clap hands
Arr. Brunt	stunt
Pub. MPH	Hand

"Clarinet Polka"
Pub. Kjos
Rubank	Clef Sign
Vitak	Clarinet

"Clementine"
Traditional
Arr. Walters-Book	Pick
Pub. Rubank	Mule

"Cold Cold Heart"
Pub. Leonard	Igloo
	Heart and
	Icicles

"Columbia the Gem of the Ocean"
Traditional
Pub. Barnhouse
Briegel
Carl Fischer
Kjos
Presser	Flag
Rubank	Shield - "U.S."

"Come Josephine in My Flying Machine"*
	Plane (old)

"Come Ona' My House"
Pub. Leonard	House

"Come Ye Thankful People, Come"
Pub. Fox	Church
Rubank	Cross

"Comrades"
Pub. Carl Fischer
Kjos	Gun
Rubank	"USA"

"Concert in the Park"
Friend	Bandstand
Arr. Teague	Podium
Pub. MPH	Tree

"Copenhagen"
Davis	Gingerbread
Pub. Morris-Book	Boy
	House
	Windmill

"Cottage for Sale" *
W. Robinson	House

"Cross Over the Bridge"
Arr. Gass
Pub. Hansen	Bridge

"Cruising Down the River"
Beadell
Arr. Yoder	Boat
Pub. Worack	Canoe

"Crusader's Hymn"
Traditional	Church
Pub. Kjos	Cross

"Cry"
Pub. Leonard	Face (sad)

"Cuban Love Song"
Stothart-McHugh	Maracas
Pub. Big 3	Sombrero

"Cuddle Up a Little Closer"
Hoschna
Arr. Halle	Two Hearts
Pub. MPH	Cuddling

"Daddy"
Troup	Dad
Arr. Yoder	Dollar Sign
Pub. Republic	Man's Face

"Daisey Bell"
Dacre
Pub. Ascher
Kjos
Leeds	Bicycle

"Dance of the Sugar Plum Fairy" (Quarto)
Tschaikowsky
Pub. Belwin	Christmas Tree

"Dancing Doll" (Octavo)
Pub. Carl Fischer	Dance Routine
	Doll

"Dancing in the Dark"
(Octavo)
Schwartz — Dance Drill
Arr. Yoder — with cap
Pub. MPH — lights

"Danny Boy" (Londonderry
Air)
Pub. Ascher — Irish Harp
Rubank — Shamrock

"Darktown Strutter's Ball"
Brooks
Arr. Yoder — Minstrel Man
Pub. Big 3 — Trombone

"Darling Nellie Gray"
Hanby
Pub. Belwin
Carl Fischer — Girl

"Davy Crockett, Ballad of"
Bruns
Arr. Beeler — Coonskin Cap
Pub. Hansen — Gun

"Daybreak"
Pub. Big 3 — Sun (rising)

"Dear Hearts and Gentle
People"
Fain — Church
Pub. Morris-Book — Hearts

"Dearie" (Do You
Remember)
Pub. Leonard — Girl
— Piano

"Dear Old Girl"
Back-Morse
Arr. Briegel — Rockin' Chair
Pub. Big 3 — Stick Girl

"Deck the Halls"
Pub. Belwin — Wreath
Schirmer — Christmas Tree

"Deep in the Heart of Texas"
Swander — Cowboy Hat
Arr. Yoder — Horse Shoe
Pub. Southern — State

"Deep Purple"
DeRose
Arr. Leidzen
Pub. Big 3 — Caplight Drill

"Deep River"
Spiritual — Boat
Pub. Ascher — Cotton Bale
Rubank — River

"Diamonds Are a Girl's
Best Friend"
Styne — Diamond
Pub. Morris — Ring

"Diane"
Rapee-Pollack
Arr. Warrington — Eiffel Tower
Pub. Big 3 — Girl

"Did Your Mother Come
from Ireland" *
— Harp
— Shamrock

"Diga Diga Do"*
J. McHugh — Nose (Durante)

"Dinah"
Akst
Arr. Lang — Eyes
Pub. Mills — Steamboat

"Doctor, Lawyer, Indian
Chief"*
Carmichael — Bow and Arrow
— Tomahawk
— Wigwam

"Doggy in the Window"
Pub. Leonard — Dog in Frame

"Doin' What Comes
Naturally"
Berlin
Arr. Leidzen
Pub. Berlin — Hillbilly House

"Donkey Serenade"
V. Herbert — Donkey
Pub. G. Schirmer — Cart

"Don't Fence Me In"
C. Porter — Bighorn Head
Arr. Teague — Boot
Pub. MPH — Cow
— Spur

"Don't Give Up the Ship"
Warren
Arr. Halle — Sailboat
Pub. MPH — Ship

"Don't Let the Stars Get
in Your Eyes"
Willet — Eyes and prop
Pub. Morris — stars
— Star

"Don't Sit Under the Apple
Tree"*
Brown — Apple
Arr. Yoder — Heart under
Pub. Robbins — Tree
— Tree

"Down Among the Sheltering
Palms"
Olman — Beach and
Arr. Schoenfeld — Umbrella
Pub. Big 3 — Palm Tree

"Down By the O-Hi-O"
Yellen — oHIo
Arr. Yoder — River
Pub. Forster — State Outline

"Down by the Station"
Arr. Lang — Engineer's Cap
Pub. Mills — Locomotive

55

"Down by the Old Mill Stream"
Taylor
Arr. Yoder
Pub. Forster — Mill Wheel

"Down in the Valley"
Pub. Kjos — Mountain

"Down the Gridiron"
Arr. Yoder — Football
Pub. Fox — Goalpost
Megaphone

"Do You Ever Think of Me"
E. Burnett
Arr. Warrington
Pub. Big 3 — Question Mark

"Doxology"
Hymn
Pub. Leonard — Church
Pro Art-Book — Cross

"Dragnet"
Pub. Hansen — Badge
Leonard — (policeman)
Gun
Novelty Stunt

"Dreams of Love"
Pub. Kjos — Heart

"Drifting and Dreaming"
Van Alstyne — Canoe
Pub. Morris — Clouds
Parachute

"Drinking Song" (Octavo)
Romberg — Beer Stein
Pub. MPH — Coca Cola
Bottle
Jug

"Drink to Me Only with Thine Eyes"
Pub. Belwin — Well Curb
Eyes

"Drums in My Heart"
Youmans
Arr. Yoder — Drum
Pub. Big 3 — Heart

"Dry Bones"
Pub. Kjos — Dog
Rubank — Skeleton
Skull and Cross
Bones

"Dying Cowboy"
Pub. Pro-Art-Book — Cowboy Hat
Cross and
Tombstone

"East of the Sun and West of the Moon"*
Bowman — Compass
Sun and Moon

"East Side, West Side" (Sidewalks of New York)
Blake — Elevated Train
Pub. Mills — Skyscraper
Rubank — Trolley Car

"Easter Parade"
Berlin — Bonnet
Arr. Leidzen — Girl
Rabbit

"Eh, Cumpari"
Pub. Leonard — Cactus
Sombrero
Solo Novelty
Stunt

"El Choclo" (Tango)
Villoldo
Pub. Ascher — Guitar
Rubank — Spanish Fan

"El Relicario"
Pub. Ascher
Kjos — Bull Ring
MPH — Mission

"Entry of the Gladiators"
Fucik
Pub. Carl Fischer — Three Rings
Kjos — Circus Tent
Rubank — Tiger Head

"Erie Canal"
Folk Song — Barge
Pub. Rubank-Book — Bridge

"Evelina"
Folk Song
Arr. Walters
Pub. Rubank-Book — Girl

"Ezekiel Saw De' Wheel"
Spiritual
Pub. Pro-Art-Book — Wheel

"Faith of Our Fathers"
Hymn
Pub. Briegel — Church
Kjos — Cross

"Far Away Places"
Pub. Leonard — Minaret
Palm Tree
Pagoda
Eiffel Tower

"Farmer in the Dell"
Traditional
Pub. Kjos — Barn
Leonard — Tractor
Schirmer — Well

"Feudin' and Fightin' "
Hillbilly Song — Gun
Pub. Chappell — Mountain
Pistol

"Fiddle Faddle" (Quarto)
Anderson
Pub. Mills — Fiddle

56

"Fine Romance, A"*

Jerome Kern	Heart

"First Noel"

Carol	Candle
Pub. Briegel	Cross
Kjos	Manger
Schirmer	Star

"Fit as a Fiddle"*

Hoffman-Goodhart

"Five Foot Two, Eyes of Blue"

Henderson	Eyes
Arr. Warrington	Stick Girl
Pub. Big 3	

"Flow Gently Sweet Afton"

Folk Song	Irish Harp
Arr. Walters	River
Pub. Rubank	Shamrock

"Forever and Ever"

Ager	Spinning Wheel

"For He's a Jolly Good Fellow"

Pub. Kjos	Hello
Rubank	Top Hat

"For Me and My Gal"

Meyer	Bell
Arr. Leaman	Stick Figure
Pub. Mills	

"Forty-Second Street" *

Dubin-Warren	Elevated Train
	Skyscraper

"Frankie and Johnnie"

Leighton-Shields	Heart
Pub. Ascher	Shot Gun

"Freddy, the Little Fir Tree" *

	Christmas Tree

"Frosty the Snowman"

Nelson-Rollins	Snowman
Pub. Leonard	

"Full Moon and Empty Arms" *

Rachmaninoff-Mossman	Moon
Arr. Yoder	Piano

Western State College Marching Band, Gunnison, Colorado
Robert Hawkins, Director. Piano Formation

"Georgia Camp Meeting"
Kerry-Mills — Cotton Bale
Pub. Hansen-Book — Minstrel Man
Marks — State Outline
Pro-Art-Book

"Georgia on My Mind" *
Carmichael — Cotton Bale
State Outline

"Girl of My Dreams"
Pub. Mills — Picture Frame
sequence
Stick Figure

"Girl that I Marry"
Berlin — Girl
Pub. Chappell — Heart
Rolling Pin
Wedding Ring

"Git Along Little Dogie"
Cowboy Song
Pub. Hansen-Book — Cowboy Hat
Leonard — Steer

"Git on Board"
Spiritual — Engineer's Cap
Arr. Yoder — Locomotive
Pub. Kjos, Quarto
Belwin-Book

"Give Me My Boots and Saddle"
Cowboy Song — Boot
Pub. Southern, N.Y. — Saddle

"Give My Regards to Broadway"
Cohan — Skyscraper
Arr. Briegel — Stage
Pub. Cohan

"Glow Worm" (Octavo)
Lincke — Firefly
Pub. Marks — Dance Step
Routine
Worm

"God Bless America"
Berlin — Shield
Pub. Berlin — "USA"
Torch of
Liberty

"God of Our Fathers"
Hymn — Church
Arr. Yoder — Cross
Pub. Kjos — Octavo
Pro-Art-Book

"Golden Earings"
Young — Cart
Pub. Famous — Crystal Ball
(globe)
Tambourine

"Goodbye My Coney Island Baby" *
Applegate — Beach and
Umbrella
Ferris Wheel
Roller Coaster

"Goodnight Irene"
Pub. Leonard — Singing Stunt

"Goodnight Ladies"
Folk Song — Lamp Post
Pub. Kjos — Moon
Southern, Texas

"Goodnight Sweetheart"
Noble-Campbell
Arr. Warrington
Pub. Big 3

"Go Fly a Kite" *
Kite

"Go Galop"
Fillmore — Circus Tent
Pub. Carl Fischer

"Goofus"
Kahn — Saxophone
Arr. Yoder
Pub. Big 3

"Go to Sleep My Baby"
Pub. Belwin — Cradle
Carl Fischer

"Graduation Day"
Pub. Hansen — School House
Diploma
Motarboard
cap

"Grandfather's Clock"
Work — Clock
Pub. Kjos
Ludwig

"Great Day"
Youmans
Arr. Yoder — Sunburst
Pub. Big 3

Grieg's Concerto"
Grieg — Piano
Wright
Pub. B. V. Conn

"Guy is a Guy, A"
Arr. Leonard — Stick Man
Pub. Leonard

"Gypsy Love Song"
Herbert — Gypsy Cart
Pub. MPH — Fiddle
Heart and
Arrow
Tambourine

58

"Hail Columbia"
Patriotic
Pub. Briegel   Shield
     Kjos   "U.S."

"Hail, Hail the Gang's All Here"
Traditional
Pub. Big 3
     Fillmore   "Hello"
     Kjos   "Hi"
     Rubank   School House

"Hail to the Chief"
Patriotic
Pub. Ascher
     Associated   Capitol
     Carl Fischer   Building
     Presser   Washington
     Rubank   Monument

"Half-As-Much"
Arr. Leonard   Broken Heart
Pub. Leonard   Drill Routine

"Hallelujah"
Youmans
Arr. Teague
Pub. MPH   Sun and Rays

"Hand Me Down My Walking Cane"
Traditional
Pub. Ascher
     Kjos   Cane

"Happy Birthday to You"
Traditional   Cake
Pub. Rubank   Numerals for
Southern, Texas   age "18",
         "21", etc.

"Happy Christmas Little Friend" *
(Christmas Seal Sale Song)
Arr. Williamson

"Happy Days Are Here Again"
Ager   Cake
Arr. Teague   Face
Pub. MPH   Political
         Symbol
         Sunburst

"Happy Holiday" *
Berlin   Cake
Pub. Berlin   Christmas Tree
         Easter Cross

"Hark, the Herald Angels Sing"
Mendelssohn   Candle
Arr. Yoder   Cross
Pub. Kjos   Christmas
         Wreath
         Note
         Angel

"Harp that Once Through Tara's Hall"
Traditional   Harp
Arr. Walters   Shamrock
Pub. Rubank   Clay Pipe

"Hawaiian Medley"
Arr. Yoder   Boat
Pub. Big 3   Grass Shack
         Palm Tree
         Stick Girl
         (hula)
         Ukulele

"Hawaiian War Chant"
Noble   Drum
Arr. Yoder   Hula Girl
Pub. Big 3   Ukulele

"Hear Dem Bells"
Traditional
Pub. Berlin—Book
Arr. Yoder   Bell
Pub. Rubank—Book   Telephone

"Heart of My Heart" *
Ryan   Heart inside
         Heart

"Heather on the Hill"
Pub. Fox   Hill
         Mountain

"Heigh Ho"
Churchill   Drill Routine
Arr. Bocker   Pick Ax
Pub. Bourne   Piston

"Here"
Arr. Leonard
Pub. Leonard   Drill Routine

"Here Comes Peter Cottontail" *
Nelson-Rolins   Basket
         Rabbit

"Here Comes Santa Claus"
Autry
Pub. Leonard   Sleigh

"Here Comes the Navy"
Oakes   Anchor
Arr. Yoder   Shield-"N"
         Ship

"Here Comes the Sun" *
Fred-Woods   Rising Sun

"Here in My Heart"
Arr. Leonard
Pub. Leonard   Heart

"He's a Jolly Good Fellow"
Traditional
Pub. Belwin
     Kjos   Cent Sign
     Leonard   Dollar Sign
     Rubank   Top Hat

"Hickory Dickory Dock"
Folk Song
Pub. Kjos
     Ludwig   Clock
     Schirmer   Mouse

"Highways Are Happy Ways"
Shay   Auto
Arr. Yoder   Intersection
Pub. Forster   Road Signs

"Hi Neighbor"
Owens   Canadian
Pub. Associated   Maple Leaf
                      Dutch Shoe
                      Mexican Hat

"Hokey Pokey"
Arr. Leonard
Pub. Leonard   Dance Routine

"Holiday For Strings" (Octavo)
Rose   Cello
Arr. Bennett   Banjo
Pub. Bregman, Vocco & Conn String Bass
                      Violin

"Home on the Range"
Cowboy Song
Pub. Ascher
     Briegel   House
     Kjos   Horse Shoe
     Rubank   Steer's Head

"Home Sweet Home"
Pub. Belwin
     Carl Fischer   House
     Leonard   Fire Place

"Honeysuckle Rose"
Fats Waller
Arr. Leonard   Drill Routine
Pub. Leonard   Rose

"Hong Kong Blues" *
Carmichael   Pagoda
                      Temple

"Hoop-De-Doo"
Arr. Yoder   Derby Hat
Pub. Frank   Hoop
                      Polka Routine

"Horse Apiece, A"
Arr. Yoder
Pub. Big 3   Horse

"Horses, Horses"
Arr. Yoder
Pub. Big 3   Horse

"Hot Time in the Old Town Tonight"
Metz
Pub. Carl Fischer
     Leonard
     Marks
     Shapiro   Moon
     Rubank   Thermometer

"How D'Ye Do Everybody"

Ascher
Pub. Belwin
     Kjos   "Hi"
     Rubank   "Hello"

"How High the Moon"
Hamilton Lewis
Pub. Chappell   Moon

"How They Gonna Keep Em Down on the Farm"
Pub. Mills   Cornstalk
                      Hog
                      Horse
                      Lamb
                      Mule

"Hymn to the Sun"
Korsakoff
Pub. Belwin-Book   Sun

"Humpty Dumpty"
(Nursery Rhyme)
Pub. Kjos   Egg

"I"
Arr. Leonard   Vocal Routine
Pub. Leonard   Stunt

"I Ain't Got Nobody" *
Williams   Head
                      Skeleton

"Idaho"
Stone
Arr. Fogelberg   Potato
Pub. Mills   State Outline

"Ida, Sweet as Apple Cider"
Munson
Arr. Briegel   Cider Jug and
Pub. Marks   Heart

"I Didn't Know What Time It Was"
Rodgers   Clock
Pub. Chappell   Alarm Clock
                      Hour Glass

"I Don't Care if the Sun Don't Shine"
Arr. Leonard   Dance Routine
Pub. Leonard   Rainbow

"I Don't Want to Set the World on Fire" *
                      World with
                      steam effect
                      (CO_2)

"If I Knew You Were A Comin' I'd a Baked a Cake"
Pub. Leonard   Cake

"I Found a Million Dollar Baby in a Five and Ten Cent Store" *
Warren   Heart and
                      Dollar Sign

"If You Knew Susie"
DeSylva
Arr. Bennett   Eye Glasses
Pub. Shapiro   Girl

"I Get a Kick Out of You" (Octavo)
Porter
Arr. Teaguè
Pub. MPH   Mule

"I Get Ideas"
Pub. Leonard   Drill Routine
"I Get the Blues When It Rains"
Stoddard   Cloud and Rain
Pub. Forster   Rainbow
"I Got Rhythm"
Gershwin   Clef
Arr. Teague   Drum
Pub. MPH   Note
                                Staff
"I Got Spurs that Jingle Jangle Jingle"
Pub. Famous   Cowboy Hat
                                Horse
                                Horse Shoe
                                Steer's Head
"I Got the Sun in the Morning"
I. Berlin
Arr. Leidzen
Pub. Berlin   Sun and Moon

"I Heard the Bells on Christmas Day"
Christmas Carol   Christmas Bell
Pub. Belwin   Christmas Tree
"I Hear Music" *
Lane   Clef
                                Note
"I Kiss Your Hand Madam"
Erwin   Girl
Arr. Teague   Hand
Pub. MPH   Heart
"I Like Mountain Music"
Weldon   Cabin
Arr. Schoenfeld   Gun
Pub. MPH   Guitar
                                Jug
                                Mountain
                                Note
                                Fiddle
                                House
                                Clef
"I'll Be Home for Christmas"
Ram   Christmas Tree
Arr. Leidzen   Fireplace
Pub. Leeds   House
"I'll Remember April"
Raye-DePaul
Arr. Johnson   Calendar
Pub. Leeds   Flower

"I'll See You in My Dreams"
Jones
Arr. Yoder   Glasses
Pub. Big 3   Heart
"I Love a Parade"
Arlen   Drill Routine
Arr. Yoder   Man-Stick
Pub. MPH   Soldier

"I Love Louisa" (Octavo)
Schwartz   Windmill
Pub. MPH   Dutch Shoe
                                Tulip
"I Love the Sunshine of Your Smile"
Pub. Leonard   Face
                                Sun
"I Love You Truly"
Carrie Jacobs Bond
Pub. Boston   Heart
"I'm a Ding Dong Daddy"
Phil Baxter   "Daddy"
Arr. Hathaway   Steamboat
Pub. Big 3   Face
"I'm Always Chasing Rainbows"
Chopin
Arr. Yoder
Pub. Big 3   Rainbow
"I'm an Old Cowhand"
Mercer   Boat
Arr. Yoder   Hat (Western)
Pub. Big 3   Cow Horns
                                Spur
                                Steer's Head
                                Horse Shoe
                                Horse
                                Overalls
                                Saddle
**"I'm a Ramblin' Wreck
   from Georgia Tech"**
Pub. Associated
   Morris   Micrometer
"I'm Forever Blowing Bubbles"
Kellette   Bubbles
Arr. Teague   Pipe and
Pub. MPH   Balloons
"I'm Heading for the Last Round-up"
Hill   Cowboy Hat
Arr. Briegel   Horse Shoe
Pub. Shapiro   Horse
                                Steer's Head
"I'm in the Jailhouse Now" *
                                Key
"I'm Looking Over a Four Leaf Clover"
Woods
Arr. Schoenfeld
Pub. MPH   Shamrock

Green
Pub. Leonard   Clef
"In a Chinese Temple Garden" (Quarto)
Ketelbey
Pub. Belwin   Pagoda

"In a Little Red Schoolhouse"
Beeler — School
Pub. Marks — "2 X 2 = 6"
Plus and
Minus Signs

"In a Little Spanish Town"
Wayne — Fan
Pub. Big 3 — Mission (Span.)
Spanish Guitar

"In a Monastery Garden" (Octavo)
Ketelbey — Mission
Pub. MPH — Pagoda

"In an 18th Century Drawing Room" (Octavo)
Scott
Arr. Teague
Pub. MPH — Spinning Wheel

"In a Persian Market" (Quarto)
Ketelby — Camel
Pub. Belwin — Palm Tree

"Indian Boy"
Fillmore — Bow and Arrow
Pub. Carl Fischer — Tepee
Tomahawk

"Indian Dance" (Pow-Pow)
Pub. Kjos — Bow and Arrow
Wigwam
Tomahawk

"Indian Love Call" (Octavo)
Friml — Canoe
Arr. Bennett — Wigwam
Pub. MPH — Waterfall

"Indiana"
McDonald-Hanley — Barn
Arr. Briegel — Cornstalk
Pub. Shapiro — State Outline

"Indian Summer" (Octavo)
Herbert — Canoe
Pub. MPH — Tepee

"In My Merry Oldsmobile"
Edwards
Arr. Teague
Pub. MPH — Auto

"In Old New York" *
Herbert — Bicycle
Old Auto
Skyscraper

"In the Evening by the Moonlight" *
Bland — Moon

"In the Good Old Summertime"
Shields-Evans — Fish
Arr. Briegel — Fishpole
Ice Cream
Cone

"In the Shade of the Old Apple Tree"
Van Alstyne — Apple
Arr. Teague — Rocking Chair
Pub. Marks — Tree

"Irish Have a Great Day Tonight"
Herbert
Pub. MPH — Shamrock

"Irish Washerwoman"
Traditional
Pub. Rubank — Shamrock

"I Saw Mommy Kissing Santa Claus"
Pub. Leonard — Fireplace
Narration
Novelty

"I Saw Stars" *
Sigler-Goodhart — Star

"Is It True What They Say about Dixie" *
Cotton Bale
Steamboat

"It Might as Well Be Spring"
Rodgers — Flower
Pub. Chappell — Rainbow

"It's a Grand Old Flag"
Pub. Cohan — Flag

"It's a Great Day for the Irish"
Edens
Arr. Teague
Pub. Big 3 — Shamrock

"It's a Hap-Hap-Happy Day" *
Sharples — Sunburst

"It's a Long Way to Tipperary"
Judge — Gun
Arr. Schoenfeld — Irish Harp
Pub. Chappell — Irish Pipe
Shamrock

"It's A Lovely Day Today" *
Berlin
Pub. Berlin — Sunburst

"It's Magic" *
Cahn-Styne — For Magician
Stunt
Stage and
Question Mark

"It's No Secret"
Arr. Leonard — Church
Pub. Leonard — Cross

"It's Only a Paper Moon"
Arlen
Arr. Teague
Pub. MPH — Moon

"It's Tulip Time in Holland"
Whiting — Dutch Shoe
Arr. Schoenfeld — Tulip
Pub. MPH — Windmill

"I've Been Workin' on the Railroad"
Pub. Bourne   Locomotive
"I've Got My Love to Keep Me Warm" *
Berlin   Heart
"I've Got Sixpence"
Folk Song
Arr. Yoder   Coin
Pub. Chappell   Coin in Purse
"I've Told Every Little Star"
Kern
Pub. Chappell   Star
"I Want a Girl"
Von Tilzer   Dad
Pub. Leonard   Heart and
     Arrow
     Rolling Pin
"I Want My Mama"
(Mama y Quero) Rhumba
Pub. Big 3   Maracas
"I Want to Be Happy" (Octavo)
Youmans
Arr. Teague
Pub. MPH   Face
"I Want to Go Back to Michigan" *
Berlin
Pub. Berlin   State Outline
"I Went to Your Wedding"
Pub. Leonard   Bells
     State Outline
"I Whistle a Happy Tune"
Rodgers
Arr. Schoenfeld   Clef
Pub. Chappell   Note
"I Wonder Who's Kissing Her Now"
Howard   Heart
Pub. Marks   Question Mark
"I, Yi, Yi, Yi, Yi, Yi, Like You
Very Much" (Samba)
Pub. Big 3   Sombrero
"Jambalaya"
Pub. Leonard   Drill Routine
"Jarabe Tapetio" (Mexican Hat Dance)
Partichela
Pub. Marks   Mexican Hat
"Japanese Sandman" *
Whiting   Pagoda
"Jeanine I Dream of Lilac Time"
Pub. Big 3   Lilac
"Jingle Bells"
Pierpont
Pub. Carl Fischer   Reindeer
    Hansen   Sleigh
    Schirmer   Icicle
"Johnson Rag" (Octavo)
Kleinkauf   Trombone
Pub. Big 3   Dance Routine

"Jolly Coppersmith"
Traditional
Pub. Ascher
    Carl Fischer
    Kjos
    Rubank   Anvil
"Jolly Old St. Nicholas"
Carol   Fireplace
Pub. Belwin   Reindeer
    Rubank   Sleigh
"Josephine"
King
Arr. Yoder
Pub. Big 3   Girl
"Joy to the World"
Handel   Candle
Pub. Belwin   Cross
    Carl Fischer   Christmas
    Kjos   Wreath
    Rubank   Manger
     Star
"June in January"
Robin
Pub. Famous   Calendar
"June Is Bustin' Out All Over"
Rodgers   Calendar
Arr. Yoder   Merry-go-round
Pub. Chappell   Sun
"Jungle Drums" (Bolero)
Lecuona
Arr. Beeler   Cooking Pot
Pub. Marks   Drum
"Just a Cottage Small
By a Waterfall" (Octavo)
Handley
Arr. Teague
Pub. MPH   House
"Just Because"
Pub. Leonard   Drill Routine
"K-K-K-Katy"
Arr. Yoder
Pub. Big 3   Girl
"Keep the Home Fires Burning"
Arr. Schoenfeld   Fireplace
Pub. Chappell   House
     Flag
"Kentucky Babe"
Buck-Geibel
Pub. Belwin—Book   Cradle
    Rubank—Book   State Outline
"Killarney"
Folk Song   Irish Harp
Pub. Rubank   Pipe
     Shamrock
"King's Horses, The"
Pub. Big 3   Crown
     Horse

63

"Kuomintang"
National Song
Pub. Kjos

"La Cumparsita" (Tango)
Rodriguez
Pub. Marks

"Lady in Red" (Rhumba)
Dickson
Arr. Lindeman
Pub. MPH

"Lady of Spain"
Evans
Pub. Fox

"La Golondrina"
Seradella
Pub. Carl Fischer
Rubank

"Lamp Is Low"
Debussy-DeRose
Arr. Yoder
Pub. Big 3

"Lamplighter's Serenade" *

"La Paloma"
Pub. Ascher
Carl Fischer

"Land of Hope and Glory" (Octavo)
Elgar
Pub. Boosey

"La Raspa" (Mexican Song)
Garcia
Pub. Pemara

"Lassas Trombone"
Fillmore
Pub. Carl Fischer

"Last Round-Up"
Arr. Yoder
Pub. Shapiro

"Last Time I Saw Paris"
Kern
Pub. Chappell

"Lazy Bones" *
Mercer-Carmichael

"Let a Smile Be Your Umbrella"
Fain
Arr. Lang
Pub. Mills

"Let It Snow, Let It Snow" *
Styne

"Let Me Call You Sweetheart"
Whitson
Arr. Yoder
Pub. Shapiro

Country Outline
(Formosa)
Rickshaw
Pagoda

Fan
Guitar

Fan
Maracas
Stick Girl

Fan
Guitar

Swallow

Lamp

Street
Lamppost

Guitar
Bird

Crown

Dance Routine
Sombrero

Trombone

Boot
Tombstone

Eiffel Tower

Fishing Pole

Face
Umbrella

Igloo
Sleigh

Heart

"Let's All Sing like the Birdies Sing"
Arr. Lang
Buchtel
Pub. Mills

"Let's Take an Old-Fashioned Walk" *
Berlin
Pub. Berlin

"Let the Rest of the World Go By"
Ball
Arr. Teague
Pub. MPH

"Let Us Gather at the Goal Line"
Arr. Schoenfeld
Pub. Big 3

"Liberty Bell March"
Sousa
Pub. Carl Fischer
Presser

"Lilacs in the Rain" *
DeRose

"Lil' Liza Jane"
Traditional
Pub. Leonard

"Limehouse Blues" (Octavo)
Braham
Arr. Teague
Pub. MPH

"Linda Mujer" (Rhumba) *

"Listen to the Mocking Bird"
Hawthorn
Pub. Mills

"Little Brown Church in the Vale"
Pitts

"Little Brown Jug"
Traditional
Pub. Belwin
Kjos
Rubank

"Little David Play on Your Harp"
Spiritual
Pub. Belwin-Book
Rubank-Book

"Little Grass Shack"
Arr. Yoder
Pub. Big 3

"Little Grey Home in the West" *

Bird
Clef
Note

Derby and Cane
Parasol

House

Football
Goalpost

Capitol
Military Cap
Shield
Statue of
Liberty
Torch of
Liberty
U.S.A.

Lilac
Umbrella
Clouds

Square Dance
Formation

Pagoda
Lamppost

Sombrero
Maracas

Bird

Church

Jug

Harp

House
Palm Tree

House
Mountains.

64

"Little Man You've Had a Busy Day" *

Wayne — Baby Crib
Rocking Horse

"Little Old Lady" *

Carmichael — Woman
Spinning Wheel

"Little Red Caboose" (Octavo)

Deke Moffit — Locomotive
Pub. Carl Fischer — Train

"Little Town of Bethlehem"

Christmas Tree
Redner — Christmas
Arr. Yoder — Wreath
Pub. Briegel — Candle
Kjos — Cross
Manger
Star

"Little White Cloud that Cried"

Ray
Pub. Leonard — Cloud

"London Bridge Is Falling Down"

Children's Song
Pub. Kjos
Schirmer — Bridge

"Long Ago and Far Away" *

Kern — Rocking Chair

"Longing for You"

Arr. Leonard — Dance Routine
Pub. Leonard — Heart

"Long, Long Ago"

Brochard — Bicycle
Pub. Belwin — Cane
and Derby
Old Auto

"Long Long Way to Tipperary"

Pub. Chappell — Shamrock

"Look to the Rainbow" *

Harburg-Lane — Rainbow

"Last April" *

DeLange-Newman — Calendar
Flower

"Lots of Coffee in Brazil" *

Jefferson — Coffee Bag
Coffee Pot

"Louise" *

Whiting — Girl

"Lou'siana Belle"

Folk Song — Cotton Bale
Arr. Walters — Girl
Pub. Rubank-Book — Steamboat
State Outline

"Louisiana Hayride" (Octavo)

Dietz-Schwartz
Arr. Teague — Hay Wagon
Pub. MPH — State Outline

"Loveliest Night of the Year"

Rosas
Arr. Schoenfeld — Star
Pub. Big 3 — Moon

"Lovely Hula Hands" *

Anderson — Hula Girl

"Lovely to Look At" *

Kern — Picture Frame

"Love Sends a Little Gift of Roses"

Openshaw
Arr. Teague — Rose
Pub. Chappell — and Heart

"Love's Old Sweet Song"

Arr. Sanders
Pub. Belwin
Kjos — Heart

"Lucky Day"

Henderson — Four Leaf
Arr. Schoenfeld — Clover
Pub. MPH — Horseshoe

"Lullaby of Broadway"

Warren — Skyscraper
Pub. MPH — Elevated Train

"Macushla"

Rowe-McMurrough
Pub. MPH — Shamrock

"Mai"

Conrad — Face and Eyes

"Make Believe" (Quarto)

Kern
Pub. Chappell — Heart

"Mama Don't Cry at My Wedding"

Arr. Leonard — Church
Pub. Leonard — Dance Routine
Ring
Cake

"Mama Inez" (Rhumba)

Arr. Beeler
Pub. Marks — Maracas

"Mambo Jambo"

Perez Prado — Mambo Dance
Pub. Leonard — Routine

"Manhattan Serenade"

Alter
Arr. Yoder — Piano
Pub. Big 3 — Skyscraper

"Man I Love" (Octavo)

Gershwin
Arr. Yoder — Man-Stick
Pub. MPH — Heart

"Man on the Flying Trapeze"
Pub. Ascher
    Big 3
    Carl Fischer
    Kjos   Circus Trapeze
    Leonard   (Swing)
    Rubank   Tent

"Man Upstairs, The"
Arr. Leonard
Pub. Leonard   Stairs

"Man with the Banjo, The"
Arr. Beeler
Pub. Hansen   Banjo

"Maple Leaf Forever"
Canadian Air   Country Outline
Pub. Carl Fischer   (Canada)
                    Maple Leaf

"March Militaire" (Octavo)
Schubert
Pub. Carl Fischer   Eiffel Tower

"March of the Majorettes"
Simon   Batons Crossed
Pub. Kjos   Boot

"Margie"
Robinson
Arr. Yoder
Pub. Mills   Girl

"Marie"
Berlin
Arr. Yoder
Pub. Berlin   Girl

"Marine's Hymn"
U. S. M. C.
Pub. Associated
    Carl Fischer
    Kjos
    Marks   Marines'
    Morris   Insignia
    Rubank   Shield-"M"

"Marseillaise"
Roger de Lisle   Eiffel Tower
Pub. Carl Fischer   Country Outline
                    (France)

"Martins and the Coys" *
Arr. Yoder   Gun
Pub. Kjos   Jug
                    Shack

"Mary Had a Little Lamb"
Nursery Rhyme
Pub. Belwin
    Schirmer   Lamb

"Mary Lou"
Lyman-Waggner
Arr. Robinson   Face
Pub. Mills   Girl

"Mary's a Grand Old Name"
Cohan
Pub. Cohan   Girl

**"May the Good Lord Bless and
Keep You" (Quarto)**
Pub. Leeds   Graduation Cap
                    Diploma
                    Class Numerals

"Melancholy Me"
Arr. Leonard
Pub. Leonard   Drill Routine

"Me and My Shadow"
Arr. Hathaway   Double Major-
Pub. Bourne   ette Routine

"Meet Me in St. Louis"
Arr. Briegel
Pub. Mills   Cotton Bale
    Vogel   Steamboat

"Meet Me Tonight in Dreamland" *
Friedman   Moon
                    Boat
                    Heart

"Memories"
Van Alstyne
Arr. Teague
Pub. MPH   Canoe

"Memphis Blues"
Handy   Cotton Bale
Arr. Briegel   Note
Pub. Handy   Trumpet

"Memphis in June" *
Carmichael   Cotton Bale
                    Steamboat

"Merry-Go-Round Broke Down"
Henderson
Arr. Schoenfeld   Merry-Go-
Pub. MPH   Round

"Mexican Hat Dance" (Octavo)
Partichela
Pub. Hansen-Book
    Marks   Sombrero

"Mexican National Hymn"
National Song
Pub. Marks   Country Outline

"Miami Beach Rhumba"
Winchell   Beach and
Arr. Beeler   Umbrella
Pub. Marks   Maracas

"Midnight in Paris"
Conrad   Eiffel Tower
Arr. Beeler   Moon
Pub. Fox   Clock

"Mighty Fortress Is Our God"
Hymn
Pub. Ascher   Cross
    Rubank   Church

"Mighty Lak' A Rose"
Nevin
Pub. Boston   Rose

"Minstrel Boy"
Irish Song
Arr. Walters
Pub. Rubank   Harp

"Missouri Waltz"
Eppel   Piano
Arr. Yoder   Steamboat
Pub. Forster   State Outline

"Mister Touchdown U.S.A."
Arr. Yoder   Football
Pub. Hansen   Helmet
      U.S.A.

"Mocking Bird Hill"
Arr. Leonard   Bird
Pub. Leonard   Hill

"Molasses, Molasses"
Arr. Leonard   Jug
Pub. Leonard   Vocal Routine
      Barrel

"Moonglow"
Hudson
Arr. Redfield
Pub. Mills   Moon

"Moon Is Low" *
Brown   Moon

"Moonlight and Roses"
Lamame-Black
Arr. Yoder   Moon
Pub. Hill & Range   Rose

"Moonlight Bay"
Wenrich   Boat
Arr. Teague   Canoe
Pub. MPH   Moon

"Moonlight Serenade"
Parish   Moon
Arr. Yoder   Clef Sign
Pub. Big 3   Note

"Moonlight Sonata"
Beethoven   Moon
Pub. Belwin-Book   Piano

"Moon Love"
Tschaikowsky-Kostelanetz
Arr. Briegel   Moon and
Pub. Famous   Heart

"Moon of Mana Koora" *
Newman   Moon and
      Palm Tree

"Moon Over Miami"
Burke   Beach and
Arr. Hathaway   Umbrella
Pub. Bourne-Book   Moon
      Palm Tree

"Moon Was Yellow" (Tango)
Ahlert   Moon
Pub. Bregman, Vocco & Conn   (cap lights)

"Morning" (Peer Gynt)
Grieg   Clock
Pub. Belwin-Book   Sun

"Mother Machree"
Irish Song   Woman
Pub. MPH

"Mule Train"
Lange-Heath   Mule
      Wagon

"Music Goes Round and Round" *
      Clef
      Lyre
      Note
      Trumpet

"Music in the Air"
Arr. Yoder   Instruments
Pub. Kjos   Clef
      Lyre
      Note
      Staff

"Music, Maestro, Please" *
Wrubel   Clef
      Lyre
      Note
      Podium

"Music, Music, Music" *
Weiss-Baum   Clef
      Lyre
      Note
      Staff

"My Cousin from Milwaukee" *
Gershwin   Beer Stein

"My Friend"
Arr. Leonard
Pub. Leonard   Cross

"My Gal Sal"
Dresser
Pub. Marks   Girl

"My Heart Belongs to Daddy" *
Porter   Heart and
      Dollar Sign

"My Heart Crys for You" *
      Heart

"My Heart Stood Still" (Octavo)
Rodgers
Arr. Teague
Pub. MPH   Heart

"My Little Girl"
Arr. Leonard
Pub. Leonard   Girl

"My Old Kentucky Home"
Foster
Pub. Kjos
    Rubank   House
    Volkwein   State Outline

"My Own United States"
Edwards
Arr. Teague
Pub. MPH   Shield

"My Shawl"
Cugat
Arr. Beeler
Pub. Marks   Mexican Cart

"My Sunny Tennessee" *
Kalmar-Raby   State Outline

"My Sweetheart's the Man in the Moon"
Pub. Leonard   Moon

"My Time Is Your Time" *
Vallee   Clock
                Hour Glass

"My Truly, Truly Fair"
Pub. Leonard   Drill Routine
                Hay Wagon

"My Wild Irish Rose"
Olcott
Arr. Teague   Shamrock
Pub. MPH   Rose

"McNamara's Band"
Pub. Vogel   Shamrock
               Stage and
                Combo

"Nancy" *
Warren   Girl

"National Emblem March"
Bagley
Pub. Mills   Shield

"New Orleans" *
Carmichael   Cotton Bale
               Steamboat

"Night and Day" (Octavo)
Porter
Arr. Yoder   Sun (change it
Pub. MPH   to Moon)

"Night Over Shanghai" *
Warren   Pagoda

"No Business like Show Business"
Berlin   Face
               Stage

"None but the Lonely Heart"
Tschaikowsky
Pub. Ascher   Heart

"No Other Love"
Rodgers
Arr. Yoder
Pub. Chappell   Heart

"Now Is the Hour"
Maori Song
Pub. Leeds   Clock

"Oh! Dem Golden Slippers"
Pub. Leonard
    Rubank   Shoe

"Oh Happy Day"
Arr. Leonard   Vocal Novelty
Pub. Leonard   Stunt

"O Holy Night"
Christmas Song   Cross
Pub. Carl Fischer   Candle
    Kjos   Manger
               Star

"Oh, How I Hate to Get Up in the Morning"
Berlin   Bugle
               Tent

"Oh Johnny Oh"
Olman
Arr. Yoder   Gun
Pub. Forster   Heart

"Oh! Susannah"
Foster
Pub Carl Fischer   Banjo
    Kjos   Covered Wagon

"Oh, You Beautiful Doll"
Ayer
Arr. Teague   Doll
Pub. MPH   Girl

"Oh, What a Beautiful Morning"
Rodgers   Cornstalk
Pub. Chappell   Sun

"Oklahoma"
Rodgers
Arr. Leidzen   Oil Derrick
Pub. Chappell   State Outline

"Old Devil Moon" *
Lane   Moon

"Old Fashioned Girl" *
Berlin   Girl

"Old Grey Mare"
Folk Song
Pub. Ascher
    Morris   Stick Horse
    Rubank   Tractor

"Old King Cole"
Nursery Rhyme
Arr. Yoder   Fiddle
Pub. Kjos   Crown

"Old MacDonald Had a Farm"
Nursery Rhyme   Cornstalk
Pub. Carl Fischer   Haystack
    Kjos   Milk Bottle
    Rubank   Pumpkin
               Tractor

"Old Man River"
Kern	Cotton Bale
Arr. Beeler	River
Pub. Chappell	River Boat

"Old Oaken Bucket"
Kailmark	Bucket
Pub. Fillmore	Pump
Ludwig	Well

"Old Paint"
Arr. Fox	Saddle
Pub. Belwin	Stick Horse

"Old Piano Roll Blues"
Pub. Leonard	Piano

"Old Refrain Waltz" (Quarto)
Kreisler	
Pub. Foley	
Hansen	Fiddle

"Old Rockin' Chair's Got Me" (Quarto)
Pub. Southern, N.Y.	Rocking Chair

"Old Spinning Wheel"
Hill	
Arr. Bennett	
Pub. Shapiro	Spinning Wheel

"Old Time Religion" *
Hymn	Church
Arr. Watters	Cross
Pub. Rubank	

"On a Slow Boat to China" *
Loesser	Boat
	Pagoda

"On a Sunday Afternoon" (Waltz)
Von Tilzer	Bicycle
Pub. Mills	Row Boat

"One Dozen Roses"
Jurgens-Donovan	
Arr. Briegel	
Pub. Famous	Rose

"One Night of Love"
Pub. Bourne-Book	Moon and
	Heart

"One O'Clock Jump" (Octavo)
Basie	
Arr. Hathaway	
Pub. Big 3	Clock

"One Rose That's Left in My Heart, The"
Pub. Shapiro	Heart
	Rose

"One World" (Octavo)
Pub. Bourne	Globe

"Only a Bird in a Gilded Cage"
Von Tilzer	Bird
	Cage

"Only a Rose"
Friml	
Arr. Briegel	
Pub. Famous	Rose

"On Miami Shore" (Waltz) *
Jacobi	Beach and
	Umbrella
	Palm Tree

"On the Alamo" *
Kahn-Jones	Mission
	Star

"On the Banks of the Wabash"
Pub. Belwin	River
Shawnee	Cornstalk

"On the Beach of Waikiki"
Pub. Big 3	Palm Tree
	Beach
	Umbrella

"On the Road to Mandalay"
Speaks	
Pub. Presser	Pagoda

"On the Sunny Side of the Street"
Bennett	
Pub. Shapiro	Sun

"On Top of Old Smoky"
Seeger	
Pub. Hansen	Guitar
Leonard	Mountain

"Onward Christian Soldiers"
Hymn	
Pub. Ascher	
Barnhouse	
Carl Fischer	
Kjos	
Presser	Cross
Volkwein	Church

"Oop-Shoop"
Arr. Leonard	
Pub. Leonard	Drill Routine

"O Solo Mio" (Waltz)
DiCapua	
Pub. Ascher	
Carl Fischer	Gondola
Kjos	Guitar

"Our Boys Will Shine Tonight"
Pub. Kjos	
Volkwein	Alumni Show

"Our Director March"
Bigelow	
Pub. Mills	Star

"Out in the Cold Again"
Koehler-Bloom	Igloo
Pub. Joy	Icicle

"Out of My Dreams" (Waltz) *
Rodgers	Heart

"Out of This Worl` *			**"Pass that Peace Pipe"**	
Arlen	World		Pub. Chappell	Pipe
	Skeleton			Tomahawk
				Tepee
"Over the Rainbow"			**"Peanut Vendor"** (Rhumba)	
Arlen			Simms	Peanut
Arr. Yoder			Pub. Marks	Sombrero
Pub. Big 3	Rainbow		**"Peggy O'Neil"** (Waltz)	
"Over the River and			Nelson-Dodge	
through the Woods"			Pub. Big 3	Girl
Traditional			**"Peg O' My Heart"**	
Arr. Walters	Sleigh		Fisher	Shamrock
Pub. Rubank-Book	Turkey		Arr. Yoder	Heart
"Over There"			Pub. Big 3	Girl
Cohan			**"Pennsylvania Polka"**	
Pub. Big 3	Cannon		Hill	Keystone
"Over the Waves"			Pub. Shapiro	State Outline
Pub. Barnhouse	Canoe		**"Pennsylvania 6-5000"** *	
Carl Fischer	Ship		Carl Sigman	Keystone
Leonard	Sailboat			Telephone
	Shield - "N"			State Outline
"Pack Up Your Troubles			**"People Will Say We're in Love"**	
in Your Old Kit Bag"			Rodgers	
Powell			Arr. Briegel	
Arr. Yoder	Bag		Pub. Chappell	Heart
Pub. Chappell	Rainbow		**"Peter, Peter, Pumpkin Eater"**	
"Pagan Love Song"			Pub. Kjos	
Brown			Leonard	Pumpkin
Arr. Yoder			**"Piano Roll Blues"**	
Pub. Big 3	Palm Tree		Pub. Leeds	Clef
"Painting the Clouds with Sunshine"				Lyre
Burke	Palette and			Note
Pub. MPH	Brush			Piano
	Sun		**"Pittsburgh, Pa."**	
"Pale Moon" (Quarto)			Pub. Leonard	Keystone
Logan	Canoe			State Outline
Pub. Forster	Moon			Skyscraper
"Pal of My Cradle Days" (Waltz) *			**"Play Fiddle Play"** (Waltz)	
Piantadosi	Cradle		Deutch	
	Tricycle		Pub. Marks	Fiddle
"Papa Won't You Dance with Me"			**"Play Gypsy, Dance Gypsy"** (Octavo)	
Styne			Kalmen	
Pub. Morris	Dance Routine		Arr. Teague	Violin
"Paper Doll"			Pub. MPH	Tambourine
Black			**"Polly Put the Kettle On"**	
Arr. Hennemann			Children's Song	
Pub. Marks	Paper Doll		Pub. Belwin	Teakettle
"Parade of the Wooden Soldiers"			**"Polonaise Militaire"**	
Jessel	Cannon		Chopin	Cannon
Arr. Beeler	Gun		Pub. Bregman, Vocco & Conn	Piano
Pub. Marks	Stick Figure		**"Pomp and Circumstance"** (Octavo)	
	Precision Drill		Elgar	Graduation
"Paris in the Spring"			Pub. Boosey	Cap
Gordon-Revel	Eiffel Tower			Diploma
Pub. Chappell	Lilac Blossom			Crown
	Calendar			

"Poor Little Rhode Island"
Styne
Pub. Shapiro-Book   State Outline

"Pop Goes the Weasel"
Traditional
Pub. Belwin
    Pro-Art
    Rubank   Pop Gun

"Potatoes Are Cheaper" *
    Money Bag
    Potato

**"Praise the Lord and
Pass the Ammunition"**
Loesser   Shield - "A"
Arr. Briegel   Shield - "N"
Pub. Famous   Cannon

"Pretend"
Arr. Leonard
Pub. Leonard   Drill Routine

"Pretty Baby"
Van Alstyne-Kahn   Cradle
Pub. MPH   Girl

"Prisoner's Song"
Massey   Key
Pub. Shapiro   Jail

"P.S. I Love You"
Arr. Leonard   Drill Routine
Pub. Leonard   Heart

"Put On Your Old Gray Bonnet"
Wenrich
Arr. Schoenfeld   Bonnet
Pub. MPH   Buggy

"Put Your Arms Around Me Honey"
Von Tilzer
Arr. Leonard   Heart
Pub. Leonard   Drill Routine

Rachmaninoff "Piano Concerto"
Rachmaninoff
Pub. Bregman, Vocco & Conn Piano

"Ragtime Cowboy Joe" *
Muir-Abrahams   Cowboy Hat
Pub. Big 3   Horse
    Horseshoe
    Steer's Head

"Rain"
Ford   Cloud
Pub. Big 3   Rain

"Rainbow 'Round My Shoulder" *
    Rainbow

"Rain on the Roof"
Ronell   House
Pub. Famous   Rain

"Ramona" (Waltz)
Wayne   Guitar
Pub. Big 3   Fan

"Ranger's Song"
Tierney
Arr. Yoder   Ranger
Pub. Big 3   Ranger's Hat

"Reachin' for the Moon" *
    Moon
    Rocket Ship

"Red River Valley"
Pourson
Pub. Ascher   Cowboy Hat
    Hansen-Book   River
    Kjos   Saddle

"Red Sails in the Sunset"
Kennedy-Gross
Arr. Briegel   Sailboat
Pub. Shapiro   Sun

"Red White and Blue"
National Song
Pub. Barnhouse   Flag
    Briegel   Shield - "U.S."
    Kjos   Statue of
    Presser   Liberty

"Remember Pearl Harbor"
Reid & Kay   Battleship
Arr. Yoder   Shield - "N"
    Plane

"Reveille"
Traditional   Bugle
Pub. Belwin   Tent
    Fillmore   Rifle

"Rhapsody in Blue" (Octavo)
Gershwin   Piano
Pub. MPH   Podium

"Rio Rita"
Tierney
Arr. Yoder
Pub. Big 3   Spanish Fan

"Rise 'n Shine"
Youmans
Arr. Teague
Pub. MPH   Sunrise

"Rock-A-By-Baby"
Nursery Rhyme
Pub. Kjos
    Leonard
    Schirmer   Cradle

"Rock-A-Bye Your Baby"
Arr. Lang   Cradle
Pub. Mills   Crooner

"Rock Around the Clock"
Max Freedman
Arr. Leonard
Pub. Leonard   Clock

"Rockin' Chair" (Quarto)
Carmichael
Pub. Southern, N.Y.   Rocking Chair

"Roll Jordan Roll"
Spiritual
Pub. Rubank
    Southern, N.Y.   River

"Rosalie"
Porter
Arr. Briegel
Pub. Chappell   Guitar

"Rose Marie, I Love You" (Octavo)
Friml
Pub. MPH   Heart

"Roses in December" *
Magidson-Oakland   Calendar
        Rose

"Roses of Picardy"
Wood
Pub. Chappell   Rose

"Row, Row, Row Your Boat"
Traditional
Pub. Kjos
    Leonard   Boat & Oars

"Rudolph, the Red-Nosed Raindeer"
Pub. St. Nicholas   Reindeer
        (stick)
        Sleigh

"Rule Brittania"
National Song
Pub. Ascher   Crown
    Carl Fisher   England
    Kjos   (outline)

"Saber Dance" (Gayne Ballet)
Pub. Leeds   Saber
Khatchaturian   Swords
Arr. Cheyette

"Sailing, Sailing"
Godfrey Marks
Pub. Carl Fischer
    Hansen   Row Boat
    Kjos   Sail Boat
    Ludwig   Ship

"St. Louis Blues"
W.C. Handy   Cotton Bale
Pub. Handy   River Boat

"San Antonio Rose"
Wills   Fan
Arr. Hathaway   Spanish
Pub. Bourne   Mission

"Santa Claus Is Coming to Town"
Coats
Arr. Yoder
Pub. Big 3   Sleigh

"Santa Lucia"
Traditional   Gondola
Pub. Ascher   Guitar
        Italy - outline

"Say It With Music" (Octavo)
I. Berlin
Arr. Yoder   Lyre
Pub. Berlin   Note

"School Days" (Waltz)
Edwards   Apple
Pub. Mills   Schoolhouse
        Seesaw
        Slide

"Seeing Nellie Home"
Traditional
Pub. Belwin   Buggy
    Kjos   Girl

"Semper Fidelis"
Sousa
Pub. Bregman, Vocco & Conn
    Carl Fischer   Marine
    Kjos   Insignia
    Rubank   Shield - "M"

"Sentimental Journey"
Green-Brown-Homer
Arr. Briegel
Pub. Morris   Trombone

"September in the Rain" *
Warren   Calendar
        Rainbow

"September Song"
Weill
Arr. Beeler   Note and Clef
Pub. Chappell   Calendar

"Serenade of the Bells"
Arr. Leonard   Mission
Pub. Leonard   Bell

"Seven Lonely Days"
Pub. Leonard   Calendar
        Novelty Stunt

"Shake, Rattle, and Roll"
Arr. Leonard
Pub. Leonard   Drill Routine

"Sh-Boom"
Pub. Leonard   Dance Routine

"Shanty in Old Shanty Town"
Siras
Pub. MPH   Shanty

"Sheik of Araby"
Snyder
Arr. Olivadoti   Camel
Pub. Mills   Tent

"She'll Be Comin' Round the Mountain"
Pub. Ascher
    Belwin
    Kjos
    Pro Art   Locomotive
    Rubank   Mountain

"She's Nobody's Sweetheart Now"
Kahn
Pub. Mills   Heart

"She May Have Seen Better Days" *

Derby and
Cane
Automobile

"She Wore a Yellow Ribbon"
Ottner
Pub. Belwin-Book   Bonnet

"Shine on Harvest Moon"
Norworth
Arr. Teague   Cornstalk
Pub. MPH   Moon

"Shortnin' Bread"
Wolfe
Pub. Kjos
Rubank-Book   Skillet

"Shoutin' Liza Trombone"
Fillmore
Pub. Carl Fischer   Trombone

"Shrimp Boats"
Howard-Weston
Pub. Hansen
Leonard   Boat

"Shuffle Off to Buffalo"
Dabin-Warren
Pub. MPH   Locomotive

"Sidewalks of New York"
Lawler
Pub. Mills   Skyscraper
Rubank   Elevated train

"Silent Night"
Gruber   Wreath
Arr. Yoder   Star
Pub. Kjos   Candle
Cross
Manger
Tree

"Silver Moon Waltz" (Octavo)
Romberg
Arr. Teague
Pub. MPH   Moon

"Singin' in the Rain"
Brown
Arr. Yoder   Umbrella
Pub. Big 3   Rain

"Sing-Sing-Sing" *
Louis Prima   Note
Clef

"Sioux City Sue" *

Girl

"Skaters' Waltz"
Waldteufel
Pub. Carl Fischer
Rubank   Skate

"Sleepy Time Gal" *
Lorenzo   Girl & Moon

"Sleigh Ride" (Octavo)
Anderson
Pub. Mills   Sleigh

"Slow Boat to China" *

Boat
Pagoda
Chinese Gate

"Small Fry" *
Carmichael   Fishing Pole

"Smile, Darn Ya, Smile"
Rich
Arr. Jones
Pub Chappell   Face

"Smiles"
Roberts
Pub. MPH   Face

"Smoke Gets in Your Eyes"
Kern
Arr. Lindemann   Cigarette
Pub. Chappell   Pipe

"Smoke Rings" *
Gifford   Cigarette
Rings

"Smokey the Bear" *

Bear
Tree

"So Beats My Heart" *
Ballard   Heart

"Somebody Love Me" (Octavo)
Gershwin
Arr. Teague
Pub. MPH   Heart

"Someday My Prince Will Come"
Pub. Bourne-Book   Crown
Sword
Horse

"Some Enchanted Evening"
Rodgers
Arr. Schoenfeld
Pub. Chappell   Moon

"Somebody Stole My Gal" *
Wood   Broken Heart

"Something about a Soldier"
Pub. Mills   Gun
Shield - "A"
Sword

"Song of India" (Octavo)
Rimsky-Korsakoff   Map
Pub. Carl Fischer   Temple

"Song of the Bayou" (Quarto)
Bloom
Pub. Big 3   Boat

"Song of the Islands"
King
Arr. Lampe
Pub. Marks   Palm Tree

Song of the Marines"
  Warren   Flag
  Arr. Halle   Gun
  Pub. MPH   Marine
                            Emblem

Song of the Vagabonds"
  Friml
  Arr. VanLoan
  Pub. Famous   Sword

Sophisticated Lady"
  Ellington
  Arr. Becker   Girl
  Pub. Mills   Skyscraper

'Sound-off"
  Arr. Yoder   Precision Drill
  Pub. Kjos   Rifle
       Shapiro   Tent
                            Bugle

'South"
  Arr. Leonard
  Pub. Leonard   Drill Routine

'South of the Border"
  Kennedy-Carr
  Arr. Briegel
  Pub. Shapiro   Sombrero

'South Rampart St. Parade"
  Haggart   Cornet
  Arr. Yoder   Man (stick
  Pub. Big 3   figure)
                            Trombone

"South Sea Island Magic"
  Pub. Joy   Palm Tree
                            Palm Hat
                            Ship

"Sparrow in Tree Top"
  Arr. Leonard   Bird
  Pub. Leonard   Tree

"Spirituals on Parade"
  Arr. Davis   Cornet
  Pub. Ludwig   Trombone
                            Musical Note

"Spring Is Here" *
  Rodgers   Flower
                            Rainbow

"Spring Song"
  Pub. Belwin
       Carl Fischer
       Cundy   Flower (note)

"Square Dance Medley"
  Arr. Heine   Cornstalk
  Pub. Fox   Fiddle
                            Haywagon
                            Square Dance
                              Routine

"Stairway to the Stars"
  Malneck-Signorelli
  Arr. Yoder   Star
  Pub. Big 3   Stairway

Michigan State University Marching Band, East Lansing, Michigan
Leonard Falcone, Director. Shooting Star Formation

"Star Dust"
Carmichael
Arr. Lang
Pub. Mills — Star

"Stars and Stripes Forever"
Sousa — Capitol
Pub. Carl Fischer — Flag
Kjos — Military Hat
Presser — Shield
Rubank — Statue of
Liberty
U.S.A.
Torch

"Stars Fell On Alabama"
Parkins — Star
Arr. Redfield — State Outline

"Stars of the Summer Night"
Arr. Yoder
Pub. Belwin
Kjos — Star

"Star Spangled Banner"
Smith
Pub. Associated
Briegel
Carl Fischer
Rubank
Schirmer
Volkwein — Shield - "U.S."

"Steam Heat"
Adler
Arr. Hill
Pub. Frank — Thermometer

"Stein Song"
Arr. R. Vallee
Pub. Carl Fischer — Beer Stein

"Stormy Weather"
Arlen
Arr. Lang — Sailboat
Pub. Mills — Ship

"Stouthearted Men"
Romberg
Arr. Yoder
Pub. MPH — Sword

"Strange Music" *
Grieg — Clef
Note
Lyre

"Strike Up the Band"
Gershwin — Cornet
Arr. Yoder — Lyre
Pub. MPH — Note
Podium
Stage

"String of Pearls"
Gray
Arr. Bungett
Pub. Chappell — Necklace

"Strummin' on the Old Banjo"
Pub. Belwin — Banjo

"Suddenly It's Spring" *
Van Hersen — Flower

"Sugar Blues"
Williams
Arr. Briegel
Pub. Leeds — Trumpet

"Sunny Side of the Street, On the"
Pub. Shapiro — Sun

"Sunny Side Up" *
DeSylva-Brown — Sun

"Sunrise Serenade" *
Carle — Rising Sun &
Note

"Surrey with the Fringe on Top"
Rodgers
Arr. Schoenfeld
Pub. Chappell — Surrey

"Swanee"
Caesar-Gershwin
Arr. Bennett — Steamboat
Pub. MPH — Cotton Bale

"Swanee River"
Foster
Pub. Kjos — River
Rubank — House (shack)

"Sweet Adeline" *
Gerard-Armstrong — Jug
Face

"Sweet Betsy from Pike"
Traditional
Pub. Belwin — Covered Wagon

"Sweet Georgia Brown"
Pinkand — Cotton Bale
Pub. MPH — State Outline

"Sweetheart of Sigma Chi"
Vernor-Stokes
Arr. Alford — Heart and
Pub. Morris — Arrow

"Sweet Leilani"
Owens
Arr. Briegel
Pub. Hansen-Book — Palm Tree

"Sweet Rosie O'Grady"
Pub. Carl Fischer — Shamrock

"Sweet Sue"
Young
Pub. Shapiro — Girl

"Swingin' in a Hammock" *
Wendling — Hammock

"Swingin' on a Star" *
Van Heusen
Arr. Burton
Pub. G. Simon — Star

75

"Swingin' on the Range"
Pub. Southern, Texas — Boat
Cowboy Hat

"Swing Low, Sweet Chariot"
Spiritual
Pub. Southern, Texas — Chariot

"Swing Medley"
("Stompin' at the Savoy")
("Sing, Sing, Sing")
Arr. Yoder — Lyre
Pub. Big 3 — Note
Staff and Clef

"Sword Dance" (Brigadoon) (Quarto)
Pub. Fox — Swords

"Syncopated Clock" (Octavo)
Parish-Anderson
Pub. Mills — Clock

**"Take Me Back to My
Boots and Saddles"**
Powell
Arr. Yoder
Pub. Southern, Texas — Boot

"Take Me Out to the Ball Game"
Von Tilzer
Arr. Morbach — Bat
Pub. Von Tilzer — Baseball

"Taps"
Traditional — Bugle
Arr. Fillmore — Tent
Pub. Carl Fischer — Moon

"Ta Ra Ra Boom Der Re"
Sayers
Pub. Hansen-Book
Mills
Rubank — Dance

"Tea for Two" (Octavo)
Youmans
Arr. Schoenfeld — Teapot
Pub. MPH — Cups

"Tennessee Waltz" (Quarto)
Redd Stewart — Dance Routine
Arr. Herfurth — Mountain
Pub. Hansen-Book — State Outline

"Tenting Tonight"
Kittredge — Cannon
Arr. Walters — Confederate
Pub. Rubank — Flag
Tent

"Thanksgiving Fantasy"
Arr. Cheyette — Church
Pub. Fox — Cross
Turkey

"Thank You for a Lovely Evening" *
Moon
Closing Time

"That Old Black Magic"
Arlen — Stage
Pub. Famous — Top Hat &
Wand

"That's an Irish Lullaby"
Shannon — Cradle
Arr. Teague — Pipe
Pub. MPH — Shamrock

"That's Where My Money Goes"
Pub. Belwin — Dollar Sign
Kjos — Uncle Sam Hat

"Them Basses"
Huffine
Pub. Carl Fischer — Tuba

"There'll Be No Teardrops Tonight"
Arr. Leonard
Pub. Leonard — Drill Routine

"There'll Be Some Changes Made"
Overstreet — For change of
Arr. Hennemann — formation
Pub. Marks — sequence

"There's a Long, Long Trail"
Elliot
Arr. Teague — Heart
Pub. MPH — Wagon

"There's Something About A Soldier"
Arr. Becker — Stick Soldier
Pub. Mills — Rifle
Cannon

"They Cut Down the Old Pine Tree" *
Ax
Tree

"Thing, The"
Pub. Leonard — Box
Novelty Stunt
Question Mark

"This Heart of Mine" *
Freed-Warren — Heart

"This Is the Army Mr. Jones"
I. Berlin — Gun
Arr. Briegel — Cannon
Pub. Berlin — Shield - "A"
Tent

"This Old House"
Pub. Leonard — House

"Three Blind Mice"
Traditional
Pub. Belwin
Pro-Art-Book
Rubank — Mice

"Three Coins in a Fountain" *
Fountain

"Three Little Fishes"
Dowell
Arr. Briegel
Pub. Joy — Fish

"Three O'Clock in the Morning"
(Waltz) (Octavo)
Robledo — Clock
Arr. Briegel — Hourglass
Pub. Big 3 — Lamppost
Moon

"Through the Years"
Youmans — Calendar
Pub. Big 3 — For Time
Sequence

"Tico Tico" (Octavo)
Abren
Arr. Kent
Pub. Southern, N.Y. — Maracas

"Tiger Rag"
La Rocca
Arr. Yoder — Circus Ring
Pub. Big 3 — Tiger Head

" 'Til I Waltz Again with You"
Arr. Leonard
Pub. Leonard — Dance Routine

" 'Til The Clouds Roll By" *
Cloud

" 'Til the End of Time"
Chopin-Mossman — Clock
Arr. Briegel — Hour Glass
Pub. Joy — Piano

"Time On My Hands" (Octavo)
Youmans — Clock
Pub. Big 3 — Hour Glass

"Tip Toe through the Tulips"
Dublin-Burke — Flower
Pub. MPH — Tulip
Dutch Shoe

"To A Wild Rose" (Octavo)
McDowell
Pub. Carl Fischer — Rose

"Too Young"
Pub. Leonard — Heart
Cradle

"Toreador Song"
Bizet — Toreador's Hat
Pub. Belwin — Bull Fight
Routine

"Totem Tom-Tom" *
Friml — Bow and
Arrow
Tomahawk
Wigwam

"Toyland" (Waltz) (Octavo)
Herbert
Arr. Teague — Teddy Bear
Pub. MPH — Doll

East High School Band, Sioux City, Iowa
Dale Carris, Director. Marching Soldier Formation

"Toy Trumpet" (Octavo)
Scott
Arr. Briegel
Pub. MPH   Trumpet
"Trail of the Lonesome Pine" *
                                     Tree
"Tramp, Tramp, Tramp"
Root
Pub. Kjos   Liberty Bell
     Leonard   Soldier
"Trees"
Rasbach
Pub. Schirmer   Tree
"Trumpeter's Lullaby" (Octavo)
Anderson   Trumpet
Pub. Mills   Cradle
"Tumbling Tumble Weeds"
Nolan
Arr. Yoder   Cactus
Pub. Chappell   Cowboy Hat
"Turkey in the Straw"
Traditional   Turkey
Pub. Kjos   Violin
     Rubank   Haystack
                                     Tractor
"Twelfth Street Rag"
Hill-Bowman
Arr. Wheeler   Piano
Pub. Shapiro   Skyscraper
"Twinkle, Twinkle Little Star"
Arr. Yoder
Pub. Kjos   Star
"Two Guitars"
Pub. Rubank   Guitar
"Two Hearts in 3/4 Time" (Octavo)
Stolz
Arr. Halle
Pub. MPH   Two Hearts
"Two Hearts, Two Kisses" *
Stone   Hearts
Arr. Williams
Pub. Leonard
"Two Little Girls in Blue" (Octavo)
Pub. Carl Fischer   Stick Girls
"Tzena, Tzena, Tzena"
Arr. Lang
Pub. Mills
     Leonard   Drill Routine

"Umbrella Man, The"
Cavanaugh
Arr. Teague   Rain
Pub. MPH   Umbrella
"Under a Blanket of Blue" *
Levinson   Star

"Under the Bamboo Tree" *
Cole   Tree
                                     Pagoda
"Underneath the Stars"
Spencer
Arr. Teague
Pub. MPH   Star
"Under the Willow She's Sleeping"
Foster   Cross and
Arr. Walters   Tombstone
Pub. Rubank   Tree

"Varsity Drag"
Pub. Chappell   Clarinet
                                     Clef
                                     Note
                                     Sax
"Volga Boatman"
Traditional
Pub. Kjos   Barge
     Rubank   River

"Wabash Blues"
Ringle-Meinkin   Note
Pub. Big 3   Trumpet
"Wabash Moon" (Waltz) *
Dreyer   Moon
"Wagon Wheels"
Hill-DeRose
Arr. Yoder   Covered Wagon
Pub. Shaprio   Wagon Wheel
"Waikiki"
Pub. Big 3   Palm Tree
"Waitin' for the Robert E. Lee"
Gilbert-Main   Cotton Bale
Pub. Southern, N.Y.   Riverboat
"Wait 'Til the Sun Shines Nellie"
Von Tilzer   Sun
Arr. Briegel   Stick Figure
Pub. Leonard   (girl)
"Walkin' My Baby Back Home"
Ahlert
Pub. Chappell   Baby Carriage
"Walter Winchell Rhumba" *
Morales .   Maracas
"Waltz You Saved for Me, The"
Flindt
Arr. Schultz   Heart and
Pub. Big 3   Arrow
"Washington Post"
Sousa
Pub. Bregman, Vocco & Conn
     Carl Fischer
     Kjos
     Rubank   Colonial Hat

"Waves March"
Fillmore · Boat
Pub. Carl Fischer · Shield - "N"
"Way Down Yonder in New Orleans"
Layton · Cotton Bale
Pub. Shapiro · Riverboat
· Trumpet

"Wearin' of the Green"
Traditional
Arr. Walters
Pub. Rubank · Shamrock
**"Wedding of the
Painted Doll" (Quarto)**
Brown
Arr. Yoder · Doll
Pub. Big 3 · Church
"We Gather Together"
Hymn · Church
Arr. Walters · Cross
Pub. Rubank

"We're in the Money" *
· Cash Register
· Dollar Sign
· Money Bag
"We Three Kings of Orient Are"
Arr. Yoder · Crown
Pub. Kjos · Star
· Camel
**"We Wish You
A Merry Christmas"**
Pub. Belwin · Wreath
· Tree
· Candle
"What's the Matter with Father"
Pub. MPH · Dollar Sign to
Rubank · Cent Sign
· Face
"Wheel of Fortune"
Arr. Leonard · Wheel
Pub. Leonard · Question Mark

"When Day Is Done" (Octavo)
Katscher
Arr. Yoder
Pub. MPH · Moon
**"When I Grow too Old
to Dream" (Waltz)**
Romberg
Arr. Briegel
Pub. Big 3 · Rocking Chair
**"When Irish Eyes
Are Smiling" (Waltz)**
Ball
Arr. Teague · Eyes
Pub. MPH · Shamrock

**"When It's Sleepy Time
Down South"** *
Renee · Banjo
Pub. Mills · Cotton Bale
**"When It's Springtime
in the Rockies"**
Sauer
Arr. Yoder
Pub. Big 3 · Mountain
"When It's Twilight on the Trail" *
Pub. Famous · Cowboy Hat
· Stick Horse
· Spur
**"When Johnny Comes
Marching Home"**
Lambert · Bugle
Pub. Kjos · Gun
Rubank · Man (stick
figure)
"When My Baby Smiles at Me"
Arr. Leonard · Baby Carriage
Pub. Leonard · Face
**"When the Moon Comes
Over the Mountain"**
Pub. Big 3 · Moon and
· Mountain
**"When the Red, Red Robin
Comes Bob, Bob Bobin' Along"**
Woods · Bird
Pub. Bourne-Book · (caplights)

"When the Saints Go Marching In"
Ed Redding
Arr. Leonard
Pub. Hansen-Book · Trumpet
Leonard · Vocal Novelty
Rubank · Drill Routine
"When You're Smiling" *
Arr. Becker · Face
"When You Wish upon a Star" *
Washington-Harline · Star
· Wishbone
"When You Wore a Tulip"
Werrick
Arr. Yoder
Pub. Big 3 · Tulip & Rose
**"When Yuba Plays the Rumba
on the Tuba"**
Hupfeld
Arr. Teague
Pub. MPH · Tuba
"Where Did You Get that Hat"
Sullivan
Pub. Ascher · Hat
Belwin · (change to
Kjos · several kinds)

**"Where Oh Where Has
My Little Dog Gone"**
Traditional — Dog
Arr. Walters — Question Mark
Pub. Rubank — Hot Dog &
Bun

"Whiffen Poof Song"
Arr. Yoder
Pub. Big 3 — Lamb

**"While Strolling through
the Park One Day"**
Pub. Leeds — Derby and
Cane

"Whistler and His Dog"
Pryor
Pub. Carl Fischer — Dog

"Whistle While You Work"
Churchill — Pick
Arr. Becker — Shovel
Pub. Bourne — Steam Shovel
Wheelbarrow

"White Christmas" (Octavo)
Berlin — Candle
Arr. Leidzen — Christmas Tree
Pub. Berlin — Wreath

"Who"
Kern
Arr. Schoenfeld — Question Mark
Pub. Chappell — in Heart

**"Who's Afraid of the
Big Bad Wolf" (Octavo)**
Churchill — House
Pub. Bourne — Question Mark
Wolf

"Who's Sorry Now"
Snyder
Pub. Mills — Question Mark

**"Who Threw the Overalls in
Mrs. Murphy's Chowder"**
Pub. Belwin — Overalls
Cooking Pot

"Why Don't You Believe Me"
Arr. Leonard
Pub. Leonard — Question Mark

"Winter Wonderland"
Bernard — Sleigh
Arr. Jacobs — Snowflake
Pub. Bregman, Cocco & Conn — design

**"With a Song In My Heart"
(Octavo)**
Rodgers
Arr. Teague
Pub. MPH — Notes

**"With My Eyes Wide Open
I'm Dreaming" ***
— Eyes
Face

"Without a Song"
Youmans
Arr. Yoder
Pub. Big 3 — Note

"World Is Waiting for the Sunrise"
Seitz
Arr. Yoder
Pub. Chappell — Sunrise

"Yale Boola"
Arr. Leidzen
Pub. Big 3 — Bulldog

"Yankee Doodle"
Traditional — Drum
Pub. Kjos — Uncle Sam's
Rubank — Hat
Washington
Monument

"Yankee Doodle Boy"
Cohan — Uncle Sam Hat
Pub. Cohan — Rifle

"Yankee Doodle Polka" *
Arr. Leidzen — Uncle Sam Hat

"Yellow Rose of Texas"
Don George — Star
Pub. Hansen — State Outline

"Yes Sir That's My Baby" *
Kahn-Donaldson — Face
Cradle

"Yesterdays" *
Kern — Old Auto
Derby and
Cane
Gay 90's
Fashion Show

"Yes, We Have No Bananas" *
— Banana

"You Are My Lucky Star" *
Brown — Star

"You Are My Sunshine"
Davis, Mitchell
Arr. Hal Leonard
Pub. Leonard
Southern, N.Y. — Sun

"You Belong to Me"
Arr. Leonard — Heart
Pub. Leonard — Ring

"You Made Me Love You"
Arr. Leonard
Pub. Hansen — Dance Routine
Leonard — Heart

"You Ought to Be in Pictures" *

    Suesse   Picture Frame
    Pub. MPH   Movie Camera
                       Stage

"Your Cheating Heart"

    Arr. Leonard
    Pub. Leonard   Heart

"You're a Grand Old Flag"

    Cohan   Flag
    Pub. Cohan   "U.S.A."

"You're as Pretty as a Picture" *

    McHugh   Picture Frame

"You're a Sweetheart" *

                       Heart

"You're in the Army Now"

    Traditional   Tent
    Pub. Ascher   Cannon
        Kjos   Rifle
                       Alarm Clock
                         (5:00 AM)
                       Drill Routine

"You're the Cream in My Coffee"

    Pub. Chappell   Coffee Cup
                       Coffee Pot

"Your Lonely Heart"

    Pub. Leonard   Heart

**"You've Got to be a
Football Hero"**

    Pub. Big 3   Football
                       Helmet
                       Megaphone
                       Goalpost

"You, You, You"

    Pub. Leonard   Drill Routine

**"Zing Went the Strings
of My Heart"** *

                       Heart

CHAPTER V

324 FIELD FORMATIONS WITH SUGGESTED MUSIC TITLES

1. Alarm Clock
"Are You Sleeping"
"I Didn't Know What Time
It Was"
"Sleepy Time Gal"

2. Anchor
"Blow the Man Down"
"Here Comes the Navy"
"Anchors Aweigh"

3. Angel
"Hark! The Herald Angels
Sing"

4. Anvil
"Anvil Chorus"
"Blacksmith Blues"

5. Apple
"An Apple for the Teacher"
"Big Apple"
"Apple Blossom Time"
"School Days"
"Don't Sit Under the Apple
Tree"

6. Atom
"At the Gremlin's Ball"
"Mars at Midnight"

7. Auto
"In My Merry Oldsmobile"
"Highways Are Happy Ways"

8. Ax
"They Cut Down the Old
Pine Tree"

9. Baby Buggy
"When My Baby Smiles at Me"
"Rock-A-By Baby"

PROP SPOKES

10. Badge (Policeman)
"Dragnet"

PROP
STAR

11. Bag
"Pack Up Your Troubles"

12. Banana
"Yes We Have No Bananas"

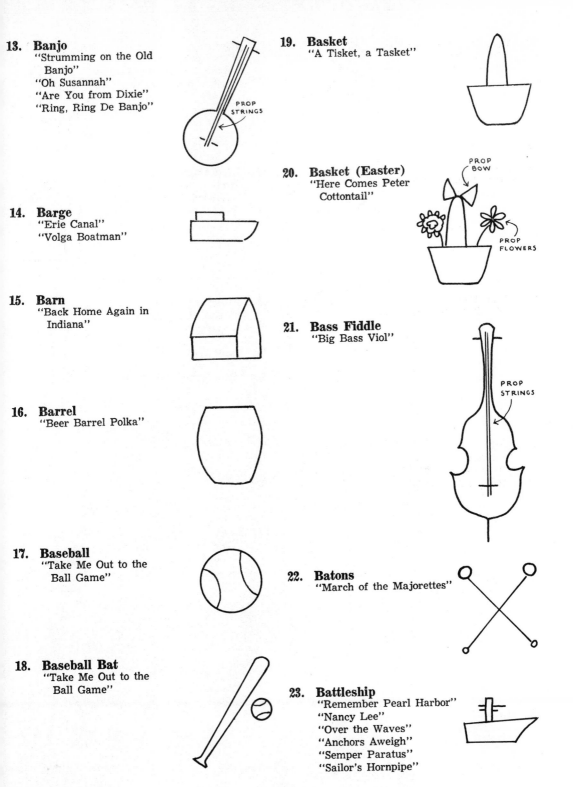

13. Banjo
"Strumming on the Old
Banjo"
"Oh Susannah"
"Are You from Dixie"
"Ring, Ring De Banjo"

PROP
STRINGS

14. Barge
"Erie Canal"
"Volga Boatman"

15. Barn
"Back Home Again in
Indiana"

16. Barrel
"Beer Barrel Polka"

17. Baseball
"Take Me Out to the
Ball Game"

18. Baseball Bat
"Take Me Out to the
Ball Game"

19. Basket
"A Tisket, a Tasket"

20. Basket (Easter)
"Here Comes Peter
Cottontail"

PROP
BOW

PROP
FLOWERS

21. Bass Fiddle
"Big Bass Viol"

PROP
STRINGS

22. Batons
"March of the Majorettes"

23. Battleship
"Remember Pearl Harbor"
"Nancy Lee"
"Over the Waves"
"Anchors Aweigh"
"Semper Paratus"
"Sailor's Hornpipe"

24. Beach and Umbrella
"By the Sea"
"Over the Waves"

25. Bear
"Bear Went Over the
Mountain"

PROP
EYE

26. Beer Stein
"My Cousin from Milwaukee"

27. Bell
"Serenade of the Bells"
"Hear Dem Bells"
"Bells of St. Mary's"

28. Bible
"Jesus Loves Me"

29. Bicycle
"Bicycle Built for Two"
("Daisy, Daisy")

PROP
SPOKES

30. Bird
"Mockingbird Hill"
"When the Red Red Robin"
"Listen to the Mocking
Bird"

PROP
EYE

31. Bird Cage
"Only a Bird in a
Guilded Cage"

32. Blunderbuss
"Thanksgiving Hymn"
"Doxolgy"

33. Boat
"Row, Row, Row Your
Boat"

34. Bomb
"Sh-Boom"
"Ta-Ra-Ra-Boom-Der-Ay"

PROP
CARDS

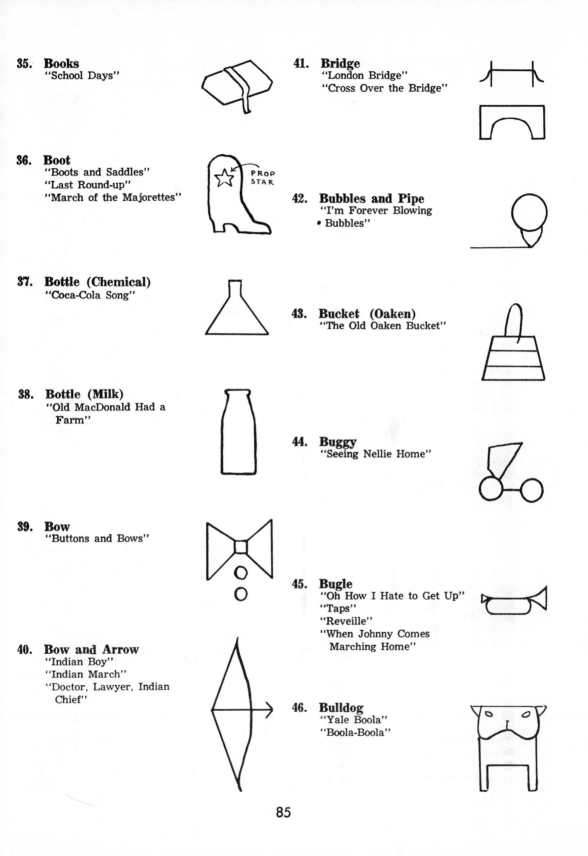

35. Books
"School Days"

36. Boot
"Boots and Saddles"
"Last Round-up"
"March of the Majorettes"

37. Bottle (Chemical)
"Coca-Cola Song"

38. Bottle (Milk)
"Old MacDonald Had a
Farm"

39. Bow
"Buttons and Bows"

40. Bow and Arrow
"Indian Boy"
"Indian March"
"Doctor, Lawyer, Indian
Chief"

41. Bridge
"London Bridge"
"Cross Over the Bridge"

42. Bubbles and Pipe
"I'm Forever Blowing
• Bubbles"

43. Bucket (Oaken)
"The Old Oaken Bucket"

44. Buggy
"Seeing Nellie Home"

45. Bugle
"Oh How I Hate to Get Up"
"Taps"
"Reveille"
"When Johnny Comes
Marching Home"

46. Bulldog
"Yale Boola"
"Boola-Boola"

85

47. Cactus
  "Tumbling Tumbleweeds"

48. Cake
  "If I'd Known You
    Were Comin' "
  "Happy Birthday"
  "Happy Holiday"
  "Happy Days Are Here
    Again"

PROP
CANDLES

7

NUMBER
OPTIONAL

49. Calendar
  "June Is Bustin' Out All
    Over"
  "September Song"
  "September in the Rain"
  "Shine on Harvest Moon"
  "April Showers"

PROP
STRING

JUNE

PROP
CARDS

50. Camera
  "If I Had a Picture of You"
  "You're as Pretty as a
    Picture"

51. Candelabra
  "Sunshine of Your Smile"
    (for Liberace show)

52. Candle
  "Adeste Fidelis"
  "Away in a Manger"
  "First Noel"
  "Hark! The Herald Angels
    Sing"

53. Candy Cane
  "Joy to the World"
  "Little Town of Bethlehem"
  "O Holy Night"
  "Silent Night"
  "We Wish You a Merry
    Christmas"
  "Babes in Toyland"

WIND WITH
PROP STREAMERS

54. Cane
  "Charlie Is My Darling"
  "Hand Me Down My
    Walkin' Cane"

55. Cannon
  "Caisson Song"
  "Praise the Lord and Pass
    the Ammunition"
  Chopin's "Polonaise
    Militaire"

PROP
SPOKES

56. Canoe
  "Driftin' and Dreaming"
  "Over the Waves"
  "Sailing, Sailing"
  "Cruising Down the River"

57. Capitol
  "America"
  "Stars and Stripes Forever"
  "America the Beautiful"

58. Cash Register
  "We're in the Money"
  "Pennies from Heaven"
  "Sing a Song of Six Pence"
  "Potatoes Are Cheaper"

59. Cat
"Tiger Rag"
"Kitten on the Keys"
"Pussy Cat, Pussy Cat,
Where Have You Been?"

60. Cello
"The Swan" - Saint Saens

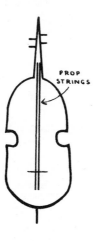

PROP STRINGS

61. Cement Mixer
"Cement Mixer Song"

62. Chair
"Old Rocking Chair's
Got Me"

63. Christmas Seal Cross
"Happy Christmas, Little
Friend"

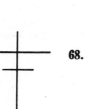

64. Christmas Tree
"Adeste Fidelis"
"Away in a Manger"
"Deck the Halls"
"Freddy, the Little Fir Tree"
"I'll Be Home for Christmas"
"I Heard the Bells on
Christmas Day"
"Silent Night"
"White Christmas"

65. Christmas Wreath
"Adeste Fidelis"
"Away in a Manger"
"Deck the Halls"
"First Noel"
"Hark! The Herald Angels
Sing"
"Little Town of Bethlehem"
"Joy to the World"
"We Wish You a Merry
Christmas"

PROP HOLLY

66. Church
"A Mighty Fortress Is
Our God"
"Come Ye Thankful People
Come"
"Crusader's Hymn"
"Doxology"
"Faith of Our Fathers"
"God of Our Fathers"
"Little Brown Church in
the Vale"
"Old Time Religion"
"Onward Christian Soldiers"
"We Gather Together"

or

67. Cigarette
"Smoke Rings"
"Smoke Gets in Your Eyes"

PROP SMOKE

68. Circus Ring
"Tiger Rag"
"Show Boy"
"Thunder and Blazes"
"Ringling Bros. Grand
Entry"

69. Circus Tent
"Go Galop"
"Entry of the Gladiators"
"Man on the Flying
   Trapeze"

70. Clarinet
"Clarinet Polka"
"Varsity Drag"

71. Clef
"Blues on Parade"
"Clarinet Polka"
"I'm Yours"
"I Whistle a Happy Tune"
"Music in the Air"
"Music Goes Round"
"Music, Music, Music"
"Music Maestro Please"
"Piano Roll Blues"
"Varsity Drag"

72. Clock
"As Time Goes By"
"Grandfather's Clock"
"Hickory Dickory Dock"
"I Didn't Know What Time
   It Was"
"Morning" (Peer Gynt)
"My Time Is Your Time"
"Syncopated Clock"
"Till the End of Time"
"Time on My Hands"

73. Clouds
"Blue Skies"
"Clouds"
"Drifting and Dreaming"
"Look for the Silver Lining"
"Little White Cloud That
   Cried"
"Till the Clouds Roll By"

74. Club (Cards)
"I'm in the Jail House Now"

75. Coffee Bag
"Lots of Coffee in Brazil"

76. Coffee Pot
"Lots of Coffee in Brazil"

77. Colonial Hat
"Washington Post"
"Turkey in the Straw"
"Yankee Doodle"
"Hail to the Chief"

78. Compass
"East Side West Side"
"Down South"
"South of the Border"
"East of the Sun, West
   of the Moon"
"Are Your from Dixie"

79. Confederate Flag
"Tenting Tonight"
"Dixie"
"Are You from Dixie"

80. Cooking Pot
"Jungle Drums"
"If I'd Known You Were
Comin' I'd a Baked a Cake"

CO₂ FIRE

83. Countries — (Outline)
National Anthems

ITALY

81. Cornstalk
"Old MacDonald Had a
Farm"
"How They Gonna Keep
Em Down on the Farm"
"Harvest Moon"

82. Cotton Bale
"Alabamy Bound"
"Waiting for the Robert
E. Lee"
"When It's Sleepy time
Down South"

84. Covered Wagon
"Sweet Betsy from Pike"
"California Here I Come"
"Oh! Susannah"

PROP SPOKES

University of Illinois Marching Band, Urbana, Illinois
Mark Hindsley, Director. Horse and Carriage Formation

85. Cowboy Hat
"Dying Cowboy"
"Deep in the Heart of
 Texas"
"I'm an Old Cowhand"
"I Got Spurs"
"I'm Headin' for the Last
 Round-up"
"Red River Valley"
"Ragtime Cowboy Joe"
"Tumbling Tumbleweeds"

86. Cradle
"Rock-a-By Baby"
"Go to Sleep My Baby"
"Kentucky Babe"

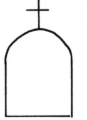

87. Cross
"Crusaders Hymn"
"Come Ye Thankful People
 Come"
"First Noel"
"Doxology"
"God of Our Fathers"
"Hark The Herald Angels
 Sing"
"Joy to the World"
"Little Town of Bethlehem"
"My Friend"
"Mighty Fortress"
"Old Time Religion"
"Onward Christian Soldiers"
"O Holy Night"
"Silent Night"
"The Old Rugged Cross"

88. Cross and Tombstone
"Dying Cowboy"

89. Crown
"We Three Kings of Orient
 Are"
"Some Day My Prince
 Will Come"
"Pomp and Circumstance"

90. Cup
"Tea for Two"

91. Dad
"Daddy"
"I'm a Ding Dong Daddy"
"I Want a Girl"

PROP EYES
AND MOUSTACHE

92. Dance Routines
(Music published with routines)

"Bunny Hop"	Bunny Hop
"Over the Waves"	Circus Performance
"Ta-Ra-Ra-Boom-Der-Ray"	Clown Dance
"Hokey, Pokey"	Hokey Pokey Routine
"I Don't Care if the Sun Don't Shine"	
"Longing for You"	Specialty
"Mamma Don't Cry at My Wedding"	Specialty
"I Wept at Your Wedding"	Specialty
"Lil Liza Jane"	Square Dance
"Tennessee Waltz"	Waltz
"Till I Waltz Again with You"	Waltz
"Auf Wiedersehen Sweetheart"	Waltz

93. Derby Hat
"The Bowery"
"Charlie Is My Darling"

94. Diamond (Cards)
"Diamonds Are a Girl's
 Best Friend"

90

95. Dog

"Doggie in the Window"
"Where Oh Where Has My Little Dog Gone"

96. Dog (Stick)

"Doggie in the Window"
"Dry Bones"
"Where Oh Where Has My Little Dog Gone"

97. Dollar Sign

"We're in the Money"
"What's the Matter with Father"
"For He's a Jolly Good Fellow"
"Oh Dem Golden Slippers"
"That's Where My Money Goes"

98. Donkey

"Donkey Serenade"
"Old Grey Mare"
"On the Trail"

99. Drill Routines

(Come With Published Tunes)
"A Guy Is A Guy"
"America on Parade"
"Boots and Saddles"
"Bonapart's Retreat"
"Botch-A-Me"
"Half As Much"
"Heigh Ho"
"Here"
"Hesitation Step"
"Honeysuckle Rose"
"I Get Ideas"
"Jambalaya"
"Just Because"
"Marching Stars and Stripes"
"My Truly Fair"
"Melancholy Me"
"Novelty Marching"
"Oop-Shoop"
"Precision Marching I, II, III"
"Precision Parade Routines
    Vol. I, II, III, IV, V."
"P.S. I Love You"
"Put Your Arms Around
    Me Honey"
"Pretend"
"Shake, Rattle, and Roll"
"South"
"There'll Be No Teardrops
    Tonight"
"Tzena, Tzena, Tzena"

100. Drum

"Drums in My Heart"
"Hawaiian War Chant"

101. Drum (Bass)

"Big Bass Drum"
"Drums in My Heart"

102. Drum (Snare)

"Drums in My Heart"
"Voodoo"

103. Dutch Shoe
  "Tip Toe through the Tulips"
  "In an Old Dutch Garden"
  "Copenhagen"

104. Egg
  "Chicken Reel"
  "Humpty-Dumpty"

105. Eiffel Tower
  "Charmaine Waltz"
  "Diane Waltz"
  "Last Time I Saw Paris"
  "Marseillaise"
  "Waltz Medley"

106. Elephant
  'Them Basses"

107. Elevated Train
  "Down by the Station"
  "Coney Island Baby"
  "Chattanooga Shoe Shine"

108. Engineer's Hat
  "Casey Jones"
  "I've Been Working on the
    Railroad"

109. Eyes
  "Beautiful Brown Eyes"
  "Dinah"
  "Charlie Is My Darling"

110. Face (Happy)
  "Happy Days Are Here
    Again"
  "Smile, Darn Ya, Smile"
  "Let a Smile Be Your
    Umbrella"

111. Face (Sad)
  "Cry"
  "I'll Cry for You"

112. Fan
  "Lady of Spain"
  "April in Portugal"

113. Feather
  "Brother Can You Spare a
    Dime"

114. Ferris Wheel
"Meet Me in St. Louis"
"Hi Ho, Come to the Fair"

115. Ferry Boat
"Over the Waves"
"By the Sea"
"Staten Island Ferry"

116. Fiddle
"Turkey in the Straw"
"Fiddle Faddle"
"Old King Cole"
"Old Refrain"
"Play Fiddle Play"

117. Firecracker
"Yankee Doodle"

118. Fireplace
"Home Sweet Home"
"Keep the Home Fires
Burning"

119. Fish
"Three Little Fishies"
"In the Good Old Summer
Time"

120. Fish Pole
"In the Good Old Summer
Time"

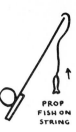

121. Flag
"America"
"America the Beautiful"
"American Patrol"
"Columbia the Gem of
the Ocean"
"Stars and Stripes Forever"

122. Flower
"Spring Song"
See listing for
Rose
Tulip
Daisy
Clover
Shamrock
Tree
Lilac

123. Football
"Football Hero"
"All American Girl"
"Betty Coed"
"Buckle Down Winsocki"

124. Football Helmet
"You Gotta Be a Football
Hero"
"Across the Field"

125. Fountain
"Three Coins in a Fountain"

93

126. Four Leaf Clover
"Lucky Day"
"I'm looking Over a Four
  Leaf Clover"

127. Gingerbread Boy
"Shortnin' Bread"
"Copenhagen"
"If I'd Known You
  Were Comin' I'd a
  Baked A Cake"

PROP
BUTTONS

128. Girl
"Alice Blue Gown"
"All American Girl"
"Betty Coed"
"Cindy"
"Charmaine"
"Darling Nellie Gray"
"Dearie"
"Diane"
"Easter Parade"
"Evelina"
"Girl that I Marry"
"If You Knew Susie"
"Josephine"
"K-K-K-Katy"
"Louisiana Belle"
"My Little Girl"
"Seeing Nellie Home"
"Waltz Medley"

or

129. Glasses (Eye)
"I'll See You in My Dreams"
"If You Knew Susie"

130. Globe (World)
"One World"

131. Goalpost
"All American Girl"
"Betty Coed"
"Buckle Down Winsocki"
"Football Hero"

132. Gondola
"Barcarolle"

133. Graduation Cap
"Pomp and Circumstance"
"Graduation Day"
"May the Good Lord Bless
  and Keep You"

134. Guitar
"Guitar Polka"
"On Top of Old Smoky"
"Old Susannah"
"Rosalie"

PROP
STRINGS

135. Gun
"Feudin' and Fightin' "
"Rangers' Song"
"When Johnny Comes
  Marching Home"
"Pistol Packin' Mamma"

136. Hammock
  "Singin' in a Hammock"

142. Hay Wagon
  'Old MacDonlad"
  "Louisiana Hayride"

137. Hand
  "Clap Yo' Hands"
  "Mammy"

138. Handcar
  "I've Been Workin' on the
  Railroad"

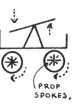

143. Heart
  "Almost like Being in
    Love"
  "A Pretty Girl"
  "Beat O' My Heart"
  "Cold, Cold Heart"
  "Drums in My Heart"
  "Girl that I Marry"
  "Goodnight Sweetheart"
  "Gypsy Love Song"
  "Heart of My Heart"
  "Here in My Heart"
  "I'm Falling in Love with
    Someone"
  "I Love You Truly"
  "I'll See You in My Dreams"
  "Let Me Call You Sweetheart"
  "Love's Old Sweet Song"
  "My Heart Cries for You"
  "My Heart Stood Still"
  "My Heart Belongs to Daddy"
  "No Other Love"
  "One Night of Love"
  "One Rose that's Left in
    My Heart"
  "Peg O' My Heart"
  "People Will Say We're in
    Love"
  "So Beats My Heart"
  "Two Hearts in ¾ Time"
  "Too Young"
  "Waltz You Saved for Me"
  "Your Lonely Heart"

139. Harp
  "It's a Long Way to
    Tipperary"
  "Lil' David Play on Your
    Harp"
  "Harp that Once thru
    Tara's Halls"
  "Minstrel Boy"

144. Hill
  "Heather on the Hill"

140. Hat
  "Where Did You Get that
    Hat?"
  See listings under:
    Cowboy Hat
    Derby
    Top Hat
    Graduation Cap
    Football Helmet
    Sombrero

145. Hog
  "How They Gonna Keep 'Em
    Down on the Farm"

141. Hay Stack
  "Old MacDonald"

95

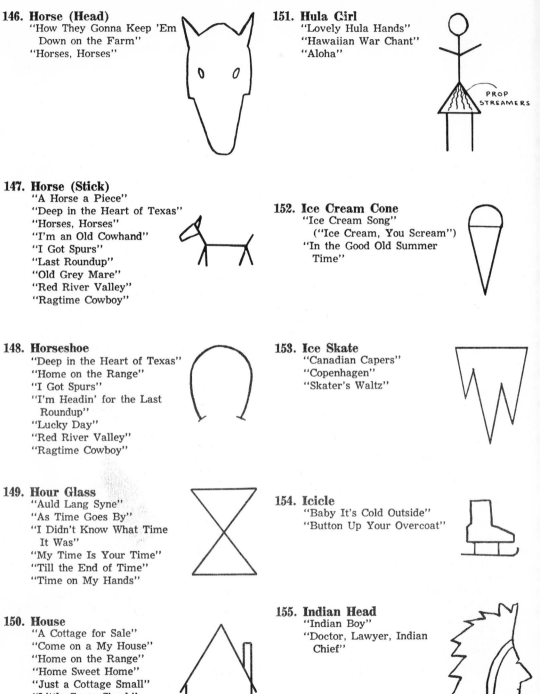

146. Horse (Head)
"How They Gonna Keep 'Em
  Down on the Farm"
"Horses, Horses"

147. Horse (Stick)
"A Horse a Piece"
"Deep in the Heart of Texas"
"Horses, Horses"
"I'm an Old Cowhand"
"I Got Spurs"
"Last Roundup"
"Old Grey Mare"
"Red River Valley"
"Ragtime Cowboy"

148. Horseshoe
"Deep in the Heart of Texas"
"Home on the Range"
"I Got Spurs"
"I'm Headin' for the Last
  Roundup"
"Lucky Day"
"Red River Valley"
"Ragtime Cowboy"

149. Hour Glass
"Auld Lang Syne"
"As Time Goes By"
"I Didn't Know What Time
  It Was"
"My Time Is Your Time"
"Till the End of Time"
"Time on My Hands"

150. House
"A Cottage for Sale"
"Come on a My House"
"Home on the Range"
"Home Sweet Home"
"Just a Cottage Small"
"Little Grass Shack"
"Little Grey Home in the
  West"
"Old Kentucky Home"
"This Old House"

151. Hula Girl
"Lovely Hula Hands"
"Hawaiian War Chant"
"Aloha"

PROP
STREAMERS

152. Ice Cream Cone
"Ice Cream Song"
  ("Ice Cream, You Scream")
"In the Good Old Summer
  Time"

153. Ice Skate
"Canadian Capers"
"Copenhagen"
"Skater's Waltz"

154. Icicle
"Baby It's Cold Outside"
"Button Up Your Overcoat"

155. Indian Head
"Indian Boy"
"Doctor, Lawyer, Indian
  Chief"

156. Instrument, Musical
"Music in the Air"
"Music, Music, Music"
"Music Maestro Please"
See Listing for:
  Bugle
  Bass Fiddle
  Banjo
  Clarinet
  Harp
  Lyre
  Maracas
  Piano
  Saxophone
  Trombone
  Tuba
  Trumpet
  Ukulele
  Violin

157. Jack-O-Lantern

158. Jet Plane
"Air Force Song"

159. Jug (Cider)
"Little Brown Jug"
"Drinking Song"

CIDER

PROP SIGN

160. Juke Box
"Juke Box Suite"
Any Pop Tune

161. Key
"I'm in the Jailhouse Now"
"Prisoner's Song"

162. Keystone
"Pittsburgh, Pa."
"Pennsylvania Polka"
"Pennsylvania 6-5000"

163. Kite
"Go Fly a Kite"

PROP STRING

PROP TAIL

164. Knife - Fork - Spoon
"Shortnin' Bread"
"If I'd Known You Were
  Coming"

165. Lamb
"How They Gonna Keep
  Em Down on the Farm"
"Mary Had a Little Lamb"
"Whiffenpoof Song"

166. Lamp
"Lamp Is Low"

167. Lamppost
"Limehouse Blues"
"Nightbeat"
"Lamp Lighter's Serenade"

168. Leaf
"Autumn Nocturne"
"Autumn Leaves"
"Autumn Serenade"
"Oh Canada"

169. Liberty Bell
"Liberty Bell March"
"Yankee Doodle"

170. Lilac
"Jeanie, I Dream of Lilac Time"
"Lilacs in the Rain"

171. Locomotive
"Alabamy Bound"
"Casey Jones"
"Chattanooga Choo-Choo"
"Down by the Station"
"Git on Board"
"She'll Be Coming Round the Mountain"
"Shuffle Off to Buffalo"

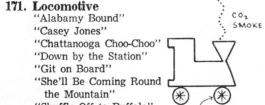

172. Lyre (Music)
"Music in the Air"
"Music Maestro Please"
"Music Goes Round"
"Music, Music, Music"
"Piano Roll Blues"
"Say it with Music"
"Swing Medley"

173. Man (Stick)
"Guy Is a Guy"
"I Love a Parade"
"Man I Love"
"Ranger's Song"
"South Rampart Street Parade"
"When Johnny Comes Marching Home Again"

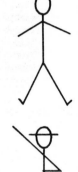

174. Manger
"Away in a Manger"
"First Noel"
"Holy Night"
"Joy to the World"
"Little Town of Bethlehem"
"Silent Night"

175. Maple Leaf
"God Save the Queen" (America)
"Oh Canada"

176. Maracas
"Bim, Bam, Bum"
"Miami Beach Rhumba"
"Mama Inez"
"Walter Winchell Rhumba"

177. Marine's Insignia (Globe and Anchor)
"Marines Hymn"
"Semper Fidelis"

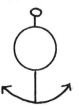

178. Megaphone
"Betty Coed"
"Football Hero"

179. Merry-Go-Round
"Merry-Go-Round Broke Down"
"The Music Goes Round"

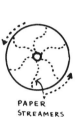

180. Metronome
"Synocopated Clock"

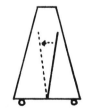

181. Mexican Cart
"Donkey Serenade"
"Chiapenecas"

182. Mice (Three Blind)
"Three Blind Mice"

183. Micrometer
"I'm a Ramblin' Wreck from Georgia Tech"

184. Military Hat
"America"
"American Patrol"
"Stars and Stripes"

185. Millwheel
"Down by the Old Mill Stream"

186. Minstrel Man
"Camptown Races"
"Darktown Strutters' Ball"
"Georgia Camp Meeting"

187. Mission (Spanish)
"When the Swallows Come Back to Capistrano"
"On the Alamo"

188. Money Bag
  "Potatoes Are Cheaper"
  "We're in the Money"

PROP
SIGN

189. Moon
  "Bali-Hai"
  "Best Things in Life Are
    Free"
  "Blue Moon"
  "By the Light of the
    Silvery Moon"
  "Carolina Moon"
  "Goodnight Ladies"
  "Hot Time in the Old Town
    Tonight"
  "In the Evening by the
    Moonlight"
  "Moon Was Yellow"
  "Moonglow"
  "Moonlight Boy"
  "Moonlight and Roses"
  "Moon Love"
  "Moon Over Miami"
  "My Sweetheart's the Man
    in the Moon"
  "Moon Is Low"
  "Moonlight Sonata"
  "One Night of Love"
  "Shine on Harvest Moon"
  "Some Enchanted Evening"

or

190. Mountain
  "Bear Went Over the
    Mountain"
  "Big Rock Candy Mountain"
  "Down in the Valley"
  "Heather on the Hill"
  "On Top of Old Smokey"
  "Springtime in the Rockies"
  "Tennessee Waltz"

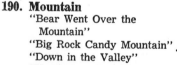

191. Mouse
  "Hickory Dickory Dock"

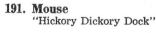

PROP
WHISKERS

192. Mouse Ears
  "Mickey Mouse March"

193. Mug (Root Beer)
  "Stein Song"

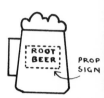

PROP
SIGN

194. Mule
  "Donkey Serenade"
  "How They Gonna Keep Em
    Down on the Farm"

195. Necklace
  "String of Pearls"

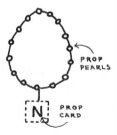

PROP
PEARLS

PROP
CARD

196. Note (Musical)
  "Blues on Parade"
  "Blowin the Blues"
  "Hark! The Herald Angels
    Sing"
  "Music in the Air"
  "Music, Music, Music"
  "Music Maestro Please"
  "Music Goes Round"
  "Piano Roll Blues"
  "Sing, Sing, Sing"
  "Swing Medley"
  "Varsity Drag"

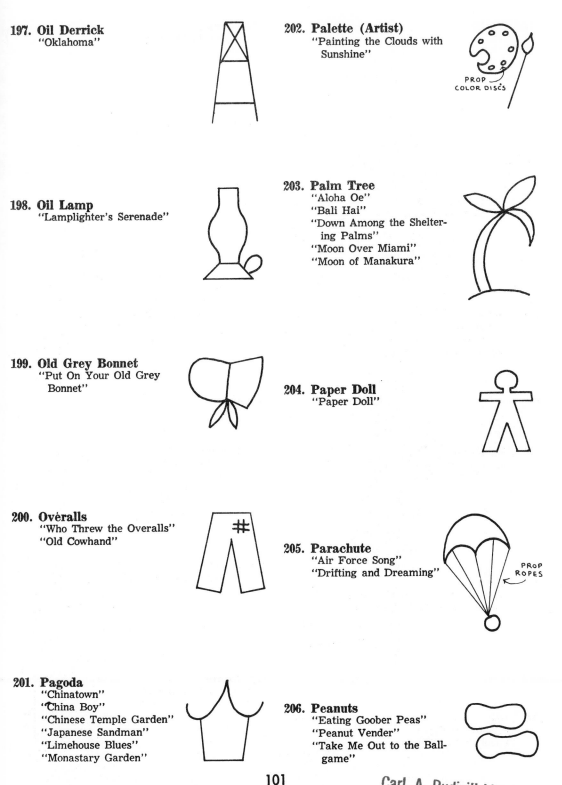

197. Oil Derrick
"Oklahoma"

198. Oil Lamp
"Lamplighter's Serenade"

199. Old Grey Bonnet
"Put On Your Old Grey Bonnet"

200. Overalls
"Who Threw the Overalls"
"Old Cowhand"

201. Pagoda
"Chinatown"
"China Boy"
"Chinese Temple Garden"
"Japanese Sandman"
"Limehouse Blues"
"Monastary Garden"

202. Palette (Artist)
"Painting the Clouds with Sunshine"

PROP
COLOR DISCS

203. Palm Tree
"Aloha Oe"
"Bali Hai"
"Down Among the Sheltering Palms"
"Moon Over Miami"
"Moon of Manakura"

204. Paper Doll
"Paper Doll"

205. Parachute
"Air Force Song"
"Drifting and Dreaming"

PROP
ROPES

206. Peanuts
"Eating Goober Peas"
"Peanut Vender"
"Take Me Out to the Ball-game"

101

207. Pennant
"Betty Coed"
"Gotta Be a Football Hero"
"Collegiate"
(any school song)
"Mr. Touchdown, U.S.A."

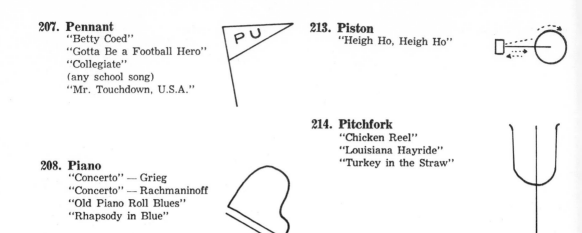

208. Piano
"Concerto" — Grieg
"Concerto" — Rachmaninoff
"Old Piano Roll Blues"
"Rhapsody in Blue"

209. Pick Ax
"Clementine"
"Heigh Ho"
"Whistle While You Work"

210. Pile Driver
"Anvil Chorus"

211. Pipe
"Pass that Peace Pipe"
"Smoke Gets in Your Eyes"

CO_2 SMOKE

212. Pistol
"Feudin' and Fightin' "
"Pistol Packin' Mamma"

213. Piston
"Heigh Ho, Heigh Ho"

214. Pitchfork
"Chicken Reel"
"Louisiana Hayride"
"Turkey in the Straw"

215. Plane (see also Jet Plane)
"Come Josephine in My
Flying Machine"
"U.S. Air Force Song"

216. Podium
"Our Director"
"Music Maestro Please"
(for presentation of guest
conductor, etc.)
"Music, Music, Music"

217. Potato
'Potatoes Are Cheaper'
"Idaho"

IDAHO

PROP
SIGN

218. Pump
"Old Oaken Bucket"

219. Pumpkin
"Old MacDonald Had a
Farm"
"Peter, Peter, Pumpkin
Eater"
"Over the River and thru
the Woods"

220. Purse
"I've Got Sixpence"

PROP
SIGN

221. Question Mark
"Can Anyone Explain"
"Thing, The"
"Where Oh Where Has My
Little Dog Gone?"
"Who's Afraid of the Big
Bad Wolf"
"Who"

222. Rabbit
"Easter Parade"
"Here Comes Peter
Cottontail"

223. Radio
"There'll Be Some Changes
Made"
"Happy Go Lucky"
(commercial themes)
"Merry Oldsmobile"
"Look Sharp March"
"See the U.S.A. in Your
Chevrolet"

224. Rain
"April Showers"
"Rain"
"Rain on the Roof"
"Singin' in the Rain"
"Umbrella Man"

225. Rainbow
"Over the Rainbow"
"Pack Up Your Troubles"
"Rainbow Round My
Shoulder"
"September in the Rain"

226. Ranger's Hat
"Ranger's Song"

227. Razor (Safety)
"Look Sharp March"

228. Red Cross
"Sisters of Mercy"
"God Bless America"

229. Reindeer (Stick)
"Jingle Bells"
"Jolly Old St. Nicholas"
"Rudolph the Red-Nosed
Reindeer"

230. Rickshaw
"China Boy"
"Chinatown My Chinatown"

PROP
SPOKES

103

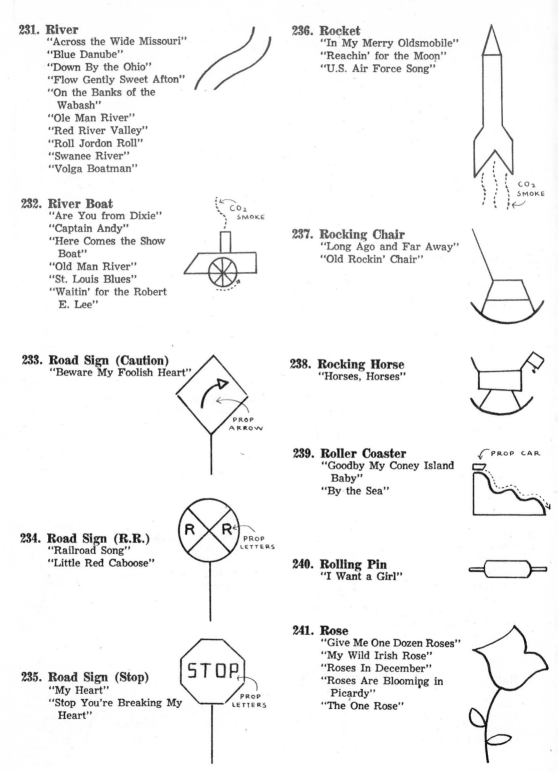

231. River
"Across the Wide Missouri"
"Blue Danube"
"Down By the Ohio"
"Flow Gently Sweet Afton"
"On the Banks of the
  Wabash"
"Ole Man River"
"Red River Valley"
"Roll Jordon Roll"
"Swanee River"
"Volga Boatman"

232. River Boat
"Are You from Dixie"
"Captain Andy"
"Here Comes the Show
  Boat"
"Old Man River"
"St. Louis Blues"
"Waitin' for the Robert
  E. Lee"

CO₂
SMOKE

233. Road Sign (Caution)
"Beware My Foolish Heart"

PROP
ARROW

234. Road Sign (R.R.)
"Railroad Song"
"Little Red Caboose"

PROP
LETTERS

235. Road Sign (Stop)
"My Heart"
"Stop You're Breaking My
  Heart"

STOP

PROP
LETTERS

236. Rocket
"In My Merry Oldsmobile"
"Reachin' for the Moon"
"U.S. Air Force Song"

CO₂
SMOKE

237. Rocking Chair
"Long Ago and Far Away"
"Old Rockin' Chair"

238. Rocking Horse
"Horses, Horses"

239. Roller Coaster
"Goodby My Coney Island
  Baby"
"By the Sea"

PROP CAR

240. Rolling Pin
"I Want a Girl"

241. Rose
"Give Me One Dozen Roses"
"My Wild Irish Rose"
"Roses In December"
"Roses Are Blooming in
  Picardy"
"The One Rose"

242. Sabre
"Sabre Dance"

243. Saddle
"Give Me My Boots and Saddle"
"I'm an Old Cowhand"
"Old Paint"
"Red River Valley"

249. Shamrock
"Harp that Once through Tara's Halls"
"Irish Washerwoman"
"Irish Have a Great Day Tonight"
"It's a Great Day for the Irish"
"Long Way to Tipperary"
"Peg O' My Heart"
"Wearin' of the Green"

244. Sailboat
"Anchors Aweigh"
"By the Sea"
"Don't Give Up the Ship"
"Over the Waves"
"Sailing, Sailing"
"Stormy Weather"

245. Sailor Hat
"Bell Bottom Trousers"
"Anchors Aweigh"
"Sailor's Hornpipe"
"Sailing, Sailing"

250. Shield - "A"
"Air Force Song"
"Praise the Lord and Pass the Ammunition"
"Something about a Soldier"
"This Is the Army Mr. Jones"
"U.S. Field Artillery"

246. Saxophone
"Goofus"
"Varsity Drag"

251. Shield - "M"
"Marines' Hymn"
"Semper Fidelis"

247. Schoolhouse
"An Apple for the Teacher"
"Graduation Day"
"School Days"

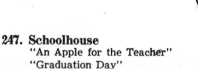

252. Shield - "N"
"Anchors Aweigh"
"Bell Bottom Trousers"
"Here Comes the Navy"
"Over the Waves"
"Praise the Lord and Pass the Ammunition"
"Remember Pearl Harbor"
"Waves March"

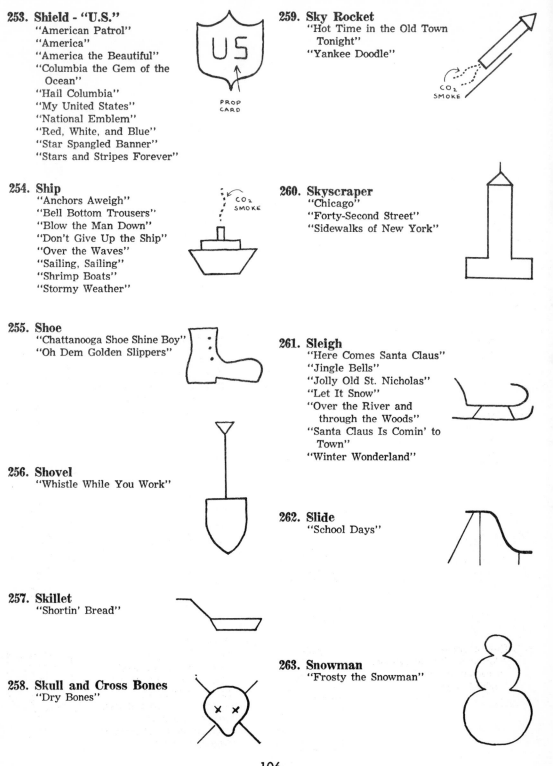

253. Shield - "U.S."
"American Patrol"
"America"
"America the Beautiful"
"Columbia the Gem of the Ocean"
"Hail Columbia"
"My United States"
"National Emblem"
"Red, White, and Blue"
"Star Spangled Banner"
"Stars and Stripes Forever"

PROP CARD

254. Ship
"Anchors Aweigh"
"Bell Bottom Trousers"
"Blow the Man Down"
"Don't Give Up the Ship"
"Over the Waves"
"Sailing, Sailing"
"Shrimp Boats"
"Stormy Weather"

CO₂ SMOKE

255. Shoe
"Chattanooga Shoe Shine Boy"
"Oh Dem Golden Slippers"

256. Shovel
"Whistle While You Work"

257. Skillet
"Shortin' Bread"

258. Skull and Cross Bones
"Dry Bones"

259. Sky Rocket
"Hot Time in the Old Town Tonight"
"Yankee Doodle"

CO₂ SMOKE

260. Skyscraper
"Chicago"
"Forty-Second Street"
"Sidewalks of New York"

261. Sleigh
"Here Comes Santa Claus"
"Jingle Bells"
"Jolly Old St. Nicholas"
"Let It Snow"
"Over the River and through the Woods"
"Santa Claus Is Comin' to Town"
"Winter Wonderland"

262. Slide
"School Days"

263. Snowman
"Frosty the Snowman"

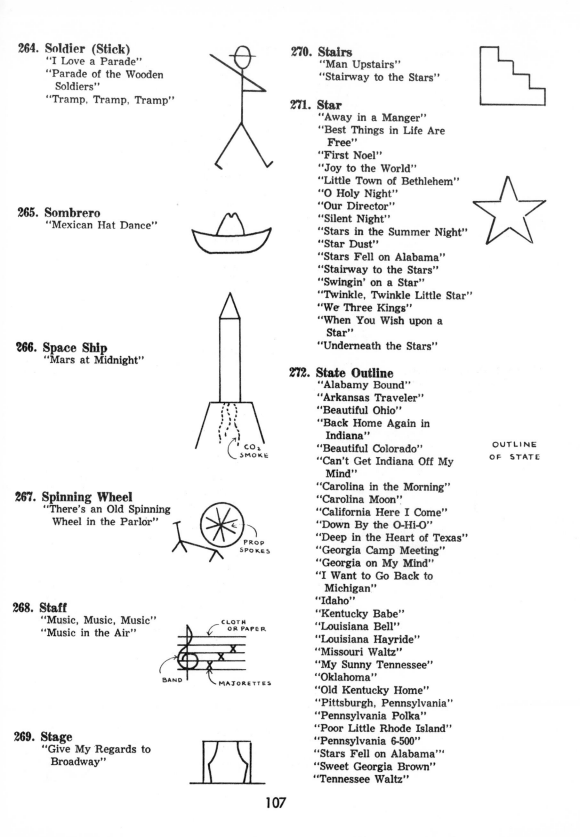

264. Soldier (Stick)
"I Love a Parade"
"Parade of the Wooden
  Soldiers"
"Tramp, Tramp, Tramp"

265. Sombrero
"Mexican Hat Dance"

266. Space Ship
"Mars at Midnight"

CO₂
SMOKE

267. Spinning Wheel
"There's an Old Spinning
  Wheel in the Parlor"

PROP
SPOKES

268. Staff
"Music, Music, Music"
"Music in the Air"

CLOTH
OR PAPER

BAND

MAJORETTES

269. Stage
"Give My Regards to
  Broadway"

270. Stairs
"Man Upstairs"
"Stairway to the Stars"

271. Star
"Away in a Manger"
"Best Things in Life Are
  Free"
"First Noel"
"Joy to the World"
"Little Town of Bethlehem"
"O Holy Night"
"Our Director"
"Silent Night"
"Stars in the Summer Night"
"Star Dust"
"Stars Fell on Alabama"
"Stairway to the Stars"
"Swingin' on a Star"
"Twinkle, Twinkle Little Star"
"We Three Kings"
"When You Wish upon a
  Star"
"Underneath the Stars"

272. State Outline
"Alabamy Bound"
"Arkansas Traveler"
"Beautiful Ohio"
"Back Home Again in
  Indiana"
"Beautiful Colorado"
"Can't Get Indiana Off My
  Mind"
"Carolina in the Morning"
"Carolina Moon"
"California Here I Come"
"Down By the O-Hi-O"
"Deep in the Heart of Texas"
"Georgia Camp Meeting"
"Georgia on My Mind"
"I Want to Go Back to
  Michigan"
"Idaho"
"Kentucky Babe"
"Louisiana Bell"
"Louisiana Hayride"
"Missouri Waltz"
"My Sunny Tennessee"
"Oklahoma"
"Old Kentucky Home"
"Pittsburgh, Pennsylvania"
"Pennsylvania Polka"
"Poor Little Rhode Island"
"Pennsylvania 6-500"
"Stars Fell on Alabama"'
"Sweet Georgia Brown"
"Tennessee Waltz"

OUTLINE
OF STATE

273. Statue of Liberty
"America"
"America the Beautiful"
"American Patrol"
"Liberty Bell March"
"Stars and Stripes Forever"

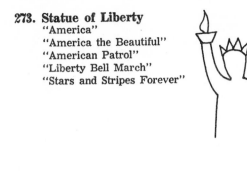

278. Stunts
"Because of You", Juke box
"Dragnet", novelty stunt
"Eh Cumpari", solo stunt
"Goodnight Irene",
    singing routine
"I", vocal
"I Saw Mummy Kissing
    Santa Claus", narrative
    novelty
"Molasses, Molasses", vocal
    novelty
"Oh Happy Day", vocal
    novelty
"Seven Lonely Days", novelty
"The Thing", novelty stunt
"When the Saints Go
    Marching In", vocal novelty
"Why Don't You Believe
    Me", vocal

274. Steam Shovel
"Whistle While You Work"

275. Steamboat Whistle
"Waiting for the Robert
    E. Lee"

279. Submarine
"Asleep in the Deep"

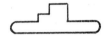

280. Sun
"Best Things in Life Are
    Free"
"Daybreak"
"Here Comes the Sun"
"Hymn to the Sun"
"I Got the Sun in
    the Morning"
"I Love the Sunshine of
    Your Smile"
"Morning" (Peer Gynt)
"On the Sunny Side of the
    Street"
"Paintin' the Clouds with
    Sunshine"
"Rise and Shine"
"Sunny Side Up"
"Wait 'Til the Sun Shines
    Nellie"
"World Is Waiting for the
    Sunrise"
"You Are My Sunshine"

or

276. Steer's Head
"Git Along Little Dogies"
"Home on the Range"
"I Got Spurs"
"I'm an Old Cowhand"
"Ragtime Cowboy. Joe"
"Red River Valley"

277. Street Lamp
"Old Lamplighter"

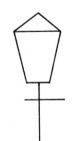

281. Sundial
"I'm Bidin' My Time"

282. Surrey
"Surrey with the Fringe on Top"

PROP SPOKES

287. Telephone
"All Alone by the Telephone"
"Hear Dem Bells"
"Pennsylvania 6-5000"

or

PROP DIAL

283. Swallow
"When the Swallows Come Back To Capistrano"

288. Tent
"Tenting Tonight"

284. Sword
"Someday My Prince Will Come"
"Sabre Dance"

289. Tepee
"Cherokee"
"Dagger Dance"
"Doctor, Lawyer, Indian Chief"
"Indian Boy"
"Indian Love Call"
"Totem Tom Tom"

CO_2 SMOKE

285. Teakettle (Teapot)
"Polly Put the Kettle on"
"Tea for Two"

286. Teddy Bear
"Toyland"
"Teddy Bear's Picnic"

PROP BUTTONS AND EYES

290. Thermometer
"Baby It's Cold Outside"
"Button Up Your Overcoat"
"Hot Time in the Old Town Tonight"
"Steam Heat"

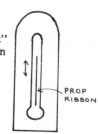

PROP RIBBON

291. Tiger (Stick Figure)
  "Tiger Rag"

292. Tiger Head
  "Tiger Rag"

293. Tomahawk
  "Cherokee"
  "Doctor, Lawyer, Indian Chief"
  "Indian Love Call"
  "Pass that Peace Pipe"

294. Top Hat
  "For He's a Jolly Good
    Fellow"

295. Torch of Liberty
  "America"
  "America the Beautiful"
  "American Patrol"
  "God Bless America"
  "Liberty Bell March"
  "Stars and Stripes Forever"

CO₂ SMOKE

296. Tractor
  "Farmer in the Dell"
  "Old Grey Mare"
  "Old MacDonald"

PROP
SPOKES

297. Trapeze
  "Man on the Flying Trapeze"

298. Tree
  "Apple Blossom Time"
  "Best Things in Life Are
    Free"
  "Don't Sit Under the Apple
    Tree"
  "Sparrow in the Tree Top"
  "Smokey the Bear"
  "They Cut Down the Old
    Pine Tree"
  "Trees"
  "Under the Willow She's
    Weeping"

or

or

299. Tricycle

PROP
SPOKES

110

300. Trolley Car
   "Clang, Clang, Clang Went
      the Trolley"

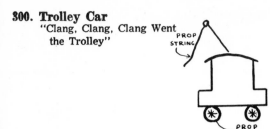

301. Trombone
   "Darktown Strutter's Ball"
   "Lassus Trombone"
   "Shoutin' Liza Trombone"
   "Twelfth Street Rag"

302. Trumpet
   "Blow Gabriel Blow"
   "Blowin' the Blues"
   "Ciribiribin"
   "Music Goes Round"
   "Trumpeter's Lullaby"
   "Sugar Blues"

303. Tuba
   "Big Joe the Tuba"
   "Them Basses"
   "When Yuba Plays the Tuba
      Down in Cuba"

304. Tulip
   "Tiptoe through the Tulips"
   "When You Wore a Tulip"

305. Turkey (Stick)
   "Turkey in the Straw"

306. T-V Set
   "Chevy Song"

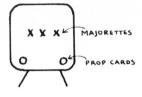

307. Ukulele
   "Hawaiian War Chant"

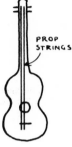

308. Umbrella
   "April Showers"
   "Lilacs in the Rain"
   "Singin' in the Rain"
   "The Umbrella Man"
   "Rain"

or

309. Uncle Sam Hat
   "Yankee Doodle"
   "Yankee Doodle Boy"
   "Yankee Doodle Polka"

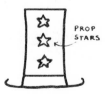

310. USA
   "America"
   "America the Beautiful"
   "American Patrol"
   "Stars and Stripes Forever"

311. Violin
"Fiddle Faddle"
"Turkey in the Straw"
"Play Fiddle Play"

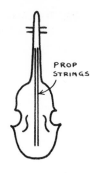

PROP STRINGS

316. Well (Well Curb)
"Drink to Me Only with
Thine Eyes"

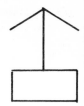

317. Wheel
"Wheel of Fortune"
"Ezekiel Saw De Wheel"

312. Volcano
"Chiapanecas"

313. Wagon Wheel
"Wagon Wheels"
"Ezekial Saw De Wheel"

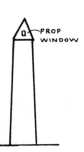

318. Wheelbarrow
"Whistle While You Work"

PROP SPOKES

319. Wigwam
"Cherokee"
"Doctor, Lawyer, Indian Chief"
"Dagger Dance"
"Indian Boy"
"Indian Love Call"

PROP WINDOW

314. Washington Monument
"Hail to the Chief"
"Yankee Doodle"

315. Wedding Ring
"Girl that I Marry"
"You Belong to Me"

PROP HEART

320. Windmill
"In an Old Dutch Garden"

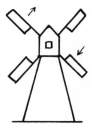

321. Wishbone
  "When You Wish upon a.
  Star"

323. Woman (Stick)
  "Alice Blue Gown"

322. Woman
  "Little Old Lady"
  "Mother Machree"

324. Worm
  "Glow Worm"

East High School Band, Sioux City, Iowa
Dale Carris, Director. Violin Formation. (See No. 311)

CHAPTER VI

PUBLISHED BAND SHOWS

Bainum-Yoder, "All Star Entrances and Fanfares", Kjos, Park Ridge 1954.

Charting and formations by Glenn Cliffe Bainum; the band arrangements are by Paul Yoder. Mr. Bainum releases for the first time some of his magnificent entrances from the Chicago "All Star Game" performances. The contents include: "All Star", "Company Front", "Cloverleaf", "Fanfare", "Combination", "Four Square", "Wheel", and "Classic Fanfares". Individual field charts are available for each performer. Conductor $1.50, parts 40 cents.

Beeler, Walter, "50 Classified Hits", Chas. Hansen, New York City, 1956.

An excellent folio in quickstep size containing standard tunes for band show use. A real gold mine. Well - arranged in a medium-easy grade. Titles are grouped in several classifications: Latin American, Dixieland, Dance Themes, Irish, Hawaiian, Holiday Music, Sea Songs, Cowboy, Modern, Waltz, Songs of the South, French, Sacred, Gay Nineties, March Trios. Conductor $1.50, band books 50¢.

Bennett, Paul, "Jamboree" Combo Band Book, Shapiro-Bernstein, New York, 1954.

A collection of 24 standard and traditional tunes in quickstep size books. Conductor (Octavo) $1.00, parts 40¢. Arranged particularly with outdoor performances in mind. Thirteen books "condensed system" of scoring. Sample titles: "By the Beautiful Sea", "There Is a Tavern in the Town", "Side by Side", "Have You Ever Been Lonely", and others.

Bergan, Hal, "Bergan's Band Shows, Vol I", Southern Music Co., San Antonio, Tex. 1950.

Five pageants for half-time use. These are published in two editions — one for 45 piece bands and another for 60 piece bands. Sets of charts for each show may be purchased separately (charts for 45 piece band 50¢; for 60 piece band 60¢) or a set of charts for the five shows may be purchased at $4 and $4.50 respectively. Music titles are suggested but no music is furnished with the charts. Excellent text material is also included on "Precision Marching", "Flash of Instruments", "Suggested Rehearsal Techniques", and "Obtaining Precision". A number of drill movements are also described. Pageant titles include the following:

"United Nations"
"Go West Young Man"
"California Here I Come"
"Homecoming"
"Oklahoma"

Bergan, Hal, "Bergan's Band Shows, Vol II", Southern Music Co., San Antonio, Texas, 1951.

Five pageants for half-time use. These are published in two editions — one for 45 piece bands and another for 60 piece bands. Sets of charts for each show may be purchased separately (charts for 45 piece band 50¢; and 60 piece band 60¢) or a set of charts for the five shows may be purchased at $4 and $4.50 respectively. Music titles are suggested but no music is furnished with the charts. Excellent text material on preparing the marching band for contest. The contest maneuvers are well explained with many suggestions for their performance with precision and flash. Also three easy novel maneuvers for the first game of the year are included. Pageant titles include:

"School Days"
"Four Freedoms"
"Thanksgiving"
"Community Chest"
"Halloween"

Bergan, Hal, "Bergan's Band Shows, Vol III", Southern Music Co., San Antonio, Texas, 1952.

Five pageants for half-time use. These are published in two editions — one for 45 piece bands and another for 60 piece bands. Sets of charts for each show may be purchased separately (charts for 45 piece band 50¢; for 60 piece band 60¢) or a set of charts for the five shows may be purchased at $4 and $4.50 respectively. Music titles are suggested, but no music is furnished with the charts. The book contains good text material on "How to Improve Your Drum Section", "Plateaus of Learning", "The Incorrect Pivot", and numerous marching band movements including "The Split Fours", "The Right Flank Reverse", "Box Flanks", etc. Titles of pageants include:

"Good Luck Pageant"
"Homecoming or Dad's Day"
"A Day in the Life of a Soldier"
"Salute to American Education Week"
"Football Pageant"

Bergan, Hal, "Band Pageantry", Music Publishers Holding Corp., N.Y., 1948.

Five half-time shows together with chapters on the marching band organization and drilling procedures. Conductor $1, band books 40¢.

Bergan, Hal, "Quickstep Band Arrangements with Formations to Go with the Music", Music Publishers Holding Corp., N.Y., 1948 and later.

Single band numbers, in which Conductor's part contains formation chart for each specific song together with some suggestions for rehearsal or performance. $1.50 each.

Titles published so far include the following:

house (cottage)	"Just a Cottage Small"
banjo	"Are You from Dixie"
star-moon	"Underneath the Stars"
ship	"Don't Give Up the Ship"
arrow thru heart	"Gypsy Love Song"
shield	"My United States"
shamrock	"Wild Irish Rose"

umbrella	"Umbrella Man"
clock	"As Time Goes By"
car (auto)	"Merry Oldsmobile"
bubble and pipe	"Forever Blowing Bubbles"
horse show	"Lucky Day"
rickshaw	"Chinatown My Chinatown"

Berryman, Joe, "Drum and Bell Lyre Interludes", Carl Fisher, 1952.

Fifteen short (16 bar) interludes for drums and bell-lyre to be used to rest the band on long parades. Also good to "scramble" on between football formations. 75¢.

Boothe, Gaedke, "Baton Twirling", W. F. Ludwig Drum Co., Chicago.

More than 175 illustrations of many variations of the twirling "fundamentals". Instructions for rehearsal of all tricks. Many advanced tricks as well as a fine collection of easy ones.

Busse, Bernard W., "Twirling Together", Hal Leonard, Winona, Minn. 1955.

A class method book for teaching unison twirling which starts with basic twirls and takes the class into field and show routines. $1.25.

Chenette-Yoder, "Another Stunt Band Folio".

Separate conductor and band parts. The folio contains sixteen comedy action and novelty numbers that can be adopted for use at football and basketball games.

Cheyette, Irving, "BVC Band Shows", Bregman, Vocco, and Conn N.Y. 1947.

Rehearsal suggestions, charts, and performance suggestions for the following formations:

grand piano	"Grieg's Piano Concerto"
grand piano	"Rachmaninoff Concerto"
grand piano	"Waves of the Danube"
cannon	"Polonaise Militaire", Chopin
marine globe and anchor	"Semper Fidelis", Sousa
sleigh	"Winter Wonderland"
colonial hat	"Washington Post", Sousa
R.O.T.C.	"High School Cadets", Sousa

Cheyette, Irving, "Thanksgiving Fantasy", Fox., N.Y. 1946.

Single number, church formation. $1.50.

Cugat, Xavier, "My Shawl".

Mexican Cart formation, single number.

Cuthbert, D. G., "Animated Band Shows", Belwin, Rockville Centre, L.I., N.Y. 1954.

Two complete shows published separately complete with music, rehearsal instructions, and performance suggestions. One formation in each show is animated. It is most effective if used with moderately high bleachers. Animated feature may be omitted if sufficient drill time not available. Music is arranged "Band-ette" (6-way) style, easy to play with cues printed on band players' parts.

No. 1 "Story of Two Alumni"
No. 2 "Vacations"
No. 3 "Men at Work"
No. 4 "Women's Work Is Never Done"

Dalby and Gregory, "Feature Spot Football Shows", Summy, Evanston, 1954.

Six complete half-time shows scored in the "six-way" style of arranging. Easy to play and well arranged for playing while marching. Also, several fanfares and entrance tunes. Show titles include:

"Seasons"

"Gilbert and Sullivan"
"Nursery Rhymes"
"Nutcracker"
"Thanksgiving"
"Homecoming"

Conductors part (1.50) includes suggested formations (some animated) and script. Parts, 50¢.

Erickson, Frank, "Fanfare, March, Cadence", Bourne, N.Y., 1953.

A selection of easy fanfares, marches and drum cadences for use at football games, basketball games and street parades. The fanfare serves as the introduction to the march. The march is usually one strain (repeated) followed by an optional drum

cadence. Conductor $1, band books 40¢. Some of the titles include:

"Cindy"
"Alouette"
"Row, Row, Row"
"Citation"
"Erickson Swing"

Evans-Heine, "Lady of Spain".

Single number with fan field formation.

Ford, Orin, "Marching and Dancing Bandsmen", Ludwig Music Co., Cleveland, Ohio, 1956.

A 24-page booklet, 8½" x 5½" to be used by the director or placed in the hands of the students. Illustrated with "footprint" cartoons to show steps and movements. The standard drill rudiments (at ease, right face, etc.) are covered in the first part of the booklet. The remaining space is given over to trick steps and dance steps. All are simple and very practical.

Ford, Orin, "Shows on Parade", Leeds, New York.

A book of shows based on popular songs. Scored in 6-way "Band-ette" style. Conductor $1.50, band books 50¢. Titles include:

"Western Show"
"Country Fair"
"Patriotic Musicians"
"Home Town Band"

Friend, Arthur, "Merry-Go-Round Broke Down".

A single number with field formation.

Griffen, Forrest, "Marching Maneuvers Bandbook", Jenkins, Kansas City, Mo., 1944.

Sixteen tunes each with a separate routine on maneuvers. Ideal for basketball use. Could be adapted for football. A separate conductor's manual outlines the procedures for performance and rehearsal. Conductor $1.00 band books 40¢.

Harr, Haskell, "Standard Rudiments and Street Beats", Ludwig Drum Co., Chicago, Illinois.

The music, which is printed on a card quickstep size, is for drums only.

Hathaway, Charles, "Quickstep Rhythms" Robbins, N.Y.C., 1953.

Fifteen standard popular tunes that have stood the test of time arranged for band. Band books are quickstep size with no formations. Conductor $1, band books 50¢.

Sample titles include:

"Johnson Rag"
"Hot Lips"
"One O'clock Jump"
"Five O'clock Jump"

Hawkins, Robert, "Hesitation Strut", Kjos Park Ridge, Illinois, 1956.

An original composition with simple and effective dance steps. Good for street, basketball, or football use. Easy, solid arrangement. Single sheet quickstep size. $2.00.

Hawkins, Robert, "Bells Up", Kjos, Park Ridge, Illinois, 1956.

A well-arranged original composition with simple flank movements and block band steps integrated into the melodic line. $2.00.

Heine, Richard, "Step with Pep", Fox, New York.

A folio of half-time show material. Quickstep size. Fifteen marches, medleys, and tunes arranged in simplified scoring for marching band use. Conductor $1.25, band books 50¢.

Herfurth-Miller-Stuart, "Halftime Hits", Pro-Art, Westbury, L.I., N.Y., 1954.

A book of eight easy field shows, complete with formations, twirling routines, and optional scripts. Separate conductor and band part books. Conductor $1.50, band books 40¢. Titles include:

1. "Spirituals"
2. "A Voyage"
3. "Two in One from Sullivan"
4. "Wilhelmina Tell"
5. "Wedding"
6. "Western Thriller"
7. "John's Other Life"
8. "Thanksgiving"

Easy grade. Effective for use at any marching appearance.

Kern, Rodgers, Youmans, et al., "Chappell Group Band Library", Chappell, N.Y., circa 1951.

Popular tunes published in quickstep size. Field formation suggested for each tune and charted for average size band. Rehearsal and performance suggestions included. $1.50 each. Titles include:

carousel	"June is Bustin' Out All Over"
calendar	"September Song"
surrey	"Oklahoma"
cactus	"Tumbling Tumbleweeds"
purse	"I've Got Sixpence"
necklace	"String of Pearls"
fan	"April in Portugal"
gun	"Feudin' and Fightin'"
shamrock	"Long Way to Tipperary"
fireplace	"Keep the Home Fires Burning"
river boat	"Ole Man River"
palm tree	"Bali Hai"
bag	"Pack Up Your Troubles in Your Old Kit Bag'

Klitz, Bill E., "Precision Parade Routines", Hal Leonard, Winona, Minn., 1952.

Street or field parade routines based on marching fundamentals. The band plays during the entire routine. All commands and executions are marked on each band part, with suggestions for rehearsal on the conductor's part. The routines are progressive in difficulty starting with No. 1 (For 48, 66, or 88 piece band). Titles issued to date include the following:

No. I "America on Parade"
No. IA "Marching Through the Years"
No. II "Over the Waves"
No. III "Marching Stars and Stripes"
No. IV "Gay Nineties Revue"

Laas, Bill, "Christmas Parade March", Belwin, Rockville Centre, L.I., N.Y. 1953. Single number with no formations. $1.25.

Titles include:

"Joy to the World"
"Deck the Halls"
"Hark, the Herald Angels Sing"
"Adeste Fidelis"
"Jingle Bells"

Laas, Bill, "Swing Time", Belwin, Rockville Centre, L.I., N.Y. 1954. $1, Bandbooks, 40¢.

Fourteen semi-original swingtunes, three swing cheers, and three swing fanfares arranged in the easy "Band-ette" (6-way) scoring. Solo choruses are optional for most instruments. Music is also usuable for combos. Conductor $1, band books 40¢. Below is a sample tune listing:

"Firehouse Frolic"
"Swanee Swing"
"Hiccup Hop"

Laas-Weber, "Director's Dilemma", Belwin, Rockville Centre, L.I., N.Y., 1953.

A single band show for the first home game or early in the season. Easy music and only two simple formations. Conductor part contains complete directions for rehearsal, script, and prop instructions. $3.00.

Laas-Weber, "SkiTime", Belwin, Rockville Centre, L.I., N.Y. 1953.

"Six Shows in Rhyme and Pantomime". Music is arranged in the 6-way "Band-ette" scoring. Several pages of instructions in the conductors manual on how to rehearse and produce the show together with some fine pictures of props and costumes. All very clever ideas in this book. Conductor $1, band books 40¢. Show titles include the formations are charted. There are some following:

"Modern Version of William Tell"
"Fearless Fanny, A Flicker Flashback"
"The Director's Dilemma"
"Story of Cowboy Joe"
"The Bullfight"
"The Bachelor Takes a Wife"

Laas-Weber, "The Story of Cowboy Joe", Belwin, Rockville Centre, L.I., N.Y., 1953.

A single band show arranged in "Band-ette" (6-way) style. This is a "skit" type show with props, two characters, and a spot for the majorettes. One band formation is included. Conductor's part has complete instructions (with pictures) for preparing props. $3.00.

Lavalle, Paul, "Band of America March", Fox, N.Y.

A marching arrangement of this solid well-known march with charted formation of "U.S." with a lyre. $2.00.

Lee, Jack, "Brigadoon", Sam Fox, N.Y., 1954.

A single half-time show based on tunes from the musical comedy "Brigadoon". It is complete with charts of four formations for marching presentations with suggested for marching presentations with suggested script and pantomime. Suggestions for rehearsal and performance are included. This is a "skit" type show with band formations. $5.50.

Tunes included are:

"Brigadoon"
"Down on MacConnachy Square"
"Sword Dance"
"Heather on the Hill"
"Almost Like Being in Love"
"Come to Me, Bend to Me"

Lee, Jack, "Halftime Shows for Band", Hal Leonard, Winona, Minn., 1951 and later.

Each show is published separately with detailed formation diagrams and procedure charts for each band memeber. The music is not difficult, with good field arrangements (cornets 2-way, clarinets 1-way, trombones 1-way, etc.). The shows are well built and have good change of pace and timing. Each show is complete with script. $4.50 for music and charts. The shows issued to date include the following:

"Latin American Saga"
"Service Salute"

"Kiddie Kapers"
"Pre-Game Band Show" (1955)
"Stephen Foster Story" (1955)
"Salute to the Scouts"
"Hillbilly Hit Parade"
"Old MacDonald's Horse"
"The Taming of the Shoe"
"The Big Top"
"Cheerleader Spotlite"
"Heart of the West"

Lee, Jack, et al., "Hal Leonard Hit Parade Series", Hal Leonard, Winona, Minn., 1950 and later.

Single issues of popular and well-known tunes, with suggested field formations for each tune by Jack Lee. Full Band $1.50.

Lee, Jack, "Mini-book of Pops for Marching", Hal Leonard, Winona, Minn., 1953,

March size, printed on card stock for use in lyres with a complete procedure chart for each bandsman. These are short episodes and can easily be included in a full length presentation. Conductor 50¢, parts 15¢. Titles include:

"The Huckleback"
"Chattanooga Shoe Shine Boy"
"Truly Truly Fair"
"I Love the Sunshine of Your Smile"

Lee, Jack, "Mini-book of Special Events Band Shows" Hal Leonard, Winona, Minn., 1953.

March size printed on card stock for use in lyres. There is a complete procedure chart for each player. These are short episodes and can easily be included in a full-length presentation. Conductor 50, parts 15. Titles include:

"Halloween"
"Dad's Day"
"Homecoming"
"Armistice Day"

Lee, Jack, "Quickie Shows", Hal Leonard Winona, Minn., 1953.

Four shows published separately (Full Band $12.50) or in books, Mini-book series (Conductor 50¢, parts 15¢ each). There

is a complete procedure chart for each bandsman. Titles are:

"Homecoming"
"Dad's Day"
"Halloween"
"Armistice Day"

Lee, Jack, "The Big Top", Hal Leonard, Winona, Minn., 1954.

A complete half-time show with a circus flavor. Included is the music and four formations. Each band part has formations printed on the back. Conductor's part contains detailed formation charts and instructions and rehearsal suggestions. Band parts are clearly cued for action.

Lee-Salmon, "Percussion Pointers for the Marching Band" Hal Leonard, Winona, Minn., 1952.

The material featuring street beats, field routines and special rhythms is practical for the school marching band. 8 percussion parts, $1.75.

Leonard, Hal, "Hal Leonard Mini-Book", Hal Leonard, Winona, Minn., 1951.

Four special event football shows, "Halloween", "Homecoming", "Dad's Day", "Armistice Day". Conductor's Book 50¢, parts 15¢. Conductor's Book contains procedure charts showing order of music, P.A. announcements, formation, and action. Arrangements are easy.

Leonard, Hal, "Parade Music No. 1", Hal Leonard, Winona, Minn., 1948.

The two fanfares, three streetbeats, and three march tunes are good for street parades and field music. The music is printed two sides on card stock for convenient lyre use.

"Leonard, Hal, Popular Standard Series" Hal Leonard, Winona, Minn.

Standard band arrangements each with suggested band formation. $1.50 each. Titles include the following:

girl	"My Little Girl"
sun	"You Are My Sunshine"
tree	"Apple Blossom Time"
boat	"Row, Row, Row"

Mesang - Thomas, "Spotlight Band Book".

Thirty-two numbers — show tunes, pop tunes, and marches. Arranged in singable keys for possible use with choirs.

Moore, Donald I., "Texas Tempo", Southern Music Publishing Co., San Antonio, Texas, 1954.

An easy 6/8 march written with the fast marching band in mind. It is good for tempos 164-196. $1.50.

Oldfield, Willis, "27 Drill Band Maneuvers" Mills, New York.

Written for schools with small enrollments using students from all grades and with large height differences. Books for students (50¢) and director ($1.50) are separate.

Ostling, Acton E., "Beverage Time", Belwin, Rockville Centre, L.I., N.Y., 1951.

A single band show release with six tunes and four formations. The conductor's part is complete with script and prop suggestions. The jug formation sequence can be cut in communities which might object. $3.00.

Ostling, Acton E., "Famous March Trios", Belwin, Rockville Centre, L.I., N.Y., 1954.

Thirty-three trios of well-known marches arranged in "Band-ette" (6 - way) style. Trios only. The keys have been changed in some instances from the original to simplify. This is good source material for football field marching. Conductor $1.00, band books 40.

Ostling, Acton E., "FasTime", Belwin, Rockville Centre, L.I., N.Y., 1956.

Thirty-two march trios and football songs

arranged with fast tempo playing in mind. Drum parts are double staffed with one part for tempi around mm-150 and the other for tempi above 172. Conductor $1.00, band books 40¢.

Ostling, Acton E., "HalfTime", Belwin, Rockville Centre, L.I., N.Y., 1953.

A collection of nine half-time shows completely worked out with the music arranged in the easy "Band-ette" (6-way) scoring. Conductor $1.00, band books 40¢.

Shows included are:

"All thru the Day"
"Music Calendar"
"Occupations"
"A Stroll through the Park"
"Gift-Time"
"Fancy Stepping"
"Precision Marching I" } may be co.
"Precision Marching II"
"Rube and Rach Quit the Band"

Ostling, Acton E., "MarchTime", Belwin, Rockville Centre, L.I., N.Y., 1952.

Fifteen well-known marches arranged in "Band-ette" (6-way) scoring for street and football use. Conductor $1.00, band books 40¢.

Ostling, Acton E., "Novelty Marching", Belwin, Rockville Centre, L.I., N.Y., 1952.

A single Band-ette (6-way) arrangement with clever steps worked into the music. Step and movement cues are on all band parts. Band stops playing and does effective flanking movements on the silent counts. $1.25.

Ostling, Acton E., "PageanTime", Belwin, Rockville Centre, L.I., N.Y., 1954.

Six pageants and three marching routines. Music arranged in "Band-ette" (t-way) scoring. Easy Grade. Conductor $1.00, band books 40¢.

Titles include:

"Weather Report"
"Hear Dem Bells"
"Songs of America"

"Books"
"Steppin Around"
"Precision Routine"
"Chopsticks on Parade"
"Marching with Style"

Ostling, Acton E., "PepTime", Belwin Rockville Centre, L.I., N.Y., 1953,

A collection of 28 marches, college songs, pop tunes and band cheers arranged for athletic event performance, in "Band-ette" (6-way) scoring. Conductor $1.00, band books 40¢.

Ostling, Acton E., "Play It with Music", Belwin, Rockville Centre, L.I., N.Y., 1951.

A single show based on a "music" idea. It contains an entrance, 4 formations and an exit. This is a complete packaged show. Conductor's part contains script and rehearsal procedure. Nò props. $3.00

Ostling, Acton E., "Precision Marching", Belwin, Rockville Centre, L.I., N.Y., 1953.

Three separate band shows (No. 1, No. 2, No. 3). Music in each is arranged in "Band-ette" (6-way) scoring. Each of these three shows has the steps, foot, and leg movements marked on the band parts. Permission is granted to mimeograph the instructions in the conductor's parts. Effective for the band that wants to get away from the formation type show. $1.25 each.

Ostling, Acton E., "Salute to Sousa", Belwin, Rockville Centre, L.I., N.Y., 1954.
A single number with formations illustrated by maneuva band pictures. Conductor's part includes very complete script with production and rehearsal instructions. Prop substitutes suggested when no public address system available. Music is in easy "Band-ette" (6-way) scoring. $3.00.

Ostling, Acton E., "Salute to Victor Herbert", Belwin, Rockville Centre, L.I., N.Y. 1955.

A melodious half-time show utilizing, as the title suggests, the tunes of Victor Herbert. The music is arranged in easy (6-way) scoring. Set of parts $3.50. Conductor's part

gives complete production instructions and also suggested script if P.A. is used. Seven field formations are illustrated by maneuva board pictures. Some of the Tunes include:

"El Dorado"
"American Girl"
"Killarney"
"Gypsy Love Song"

Ostling, Acton E., "ShowTime", Belwin, Rockville Centre, L.I., N.Y., 1953.

Eight shows and three marches arranged in the easy "Band-ette" (6-way) scoring. Formations are illustrated by maneuva-band pictures in the conductor's book. Conductor $1.00, band parts 40¢. Show titles include:

"Points of the Compass"
"Sky-Ride"
"Beverage Time"
"Red Letter Days"
"Play it with Music"

"Precision Marching" }
"Novelty Marching" } may be combined

Ostling, Acton E., "SporTime", Belwin, Rockville Centre, L.I., N.Y., 1950.

Twenty-eight marches, pep songs, and pep tunes arranged in easy "Band-ette" (6-way) scoring for use at athletic performances. Conductor $1.00, band books 40¢.

Ostling, Acton E., "StreeTime", Belwin, Rockville Centre, L.I., N.Y.

Sixteen well-known marches arranged in easy "Band-ette" (6-way) scoring for football and parade use. Conductor $1.00, band books 40¢.

Ostling, Acton E., "Twenty-nine More March Trios", Belwin, Rockville Centre, L.I., N.Y. 1956.

Another group of well-known march trios arranged in the easy to play "Band-ette" (6-way) scoring. Only 4 easy band keys are used throughout the book. Drum parts are easy to memorize for field and street use by the use of repeated figures. This is a good selection of march trios. Conductor $1.00, band books 40¢.

Ostling-Cuthbert, "StunTime", Belwin, Rockville Centre, L.I., N.Y., 1954.

Seven complete half-time shows, music arranged in the easy "Band-ette" (6-way) scoring. Formations are illustrated in the conductor's manual with maneuva band pictures. Good production notes included. Conductor $1.00, band books 40¢. Show titles include:

"Bandaze"
"Homecoming"
"School Days"
"Christmas"
"Tuney and Looney Play The Cornet"
"Goldilocks and the Three Bears"
"East Lynn 'Meller Drummer' "

Paulson, Joseph, "In Formation", Pro-Art, Westbury, L.I., N.Y., 1954.

A band folio of four complete field shows with two pre-game novelties and two fanfares. Music is arranged for field purposes. The Conductor's book contains charts and instructions. Formations are designed for the medium size band and may be adapted for street or indoor use. Conductor $1.25, band books 40¢. Half-time titles include:

1. "Precision Drill"
2. "County Fair"
3. "Swingtime"
4. "Footlight Parade"

Pre-game titles include:

1. "Friday Blues"
2. "Trombonitis"

Prescott, Gerald R., "Gridrama", Schmitt Publications, Minneapolis, Minn., 1955.

Four dramatic type football shows are combined with street parade routines, music yells for pep sessions, and a group of street beats and novelty routines for the drummers. Here is a book for the entire year. Conductor's book has production instructions and rehearsal synopsis. Suggested formations are illustrated by line drawings. Arrangements are in the 6-way scoring. Conductor $1.00, band books 40¢. Show titles include:

"Opening Game Show"
"Inside U.S.A."

"Hut - 2 - 3 - 4"
"Life in our School"
"Pre-Game Routine"

Prescott-McLeod, "Intermission", Schmitt Publications, Minneapolis, Minn., 1953.

A book of seven football shows arranged in 6-way scoring by James McLeod. Shows may be adapted for basketball or pep assembly use. Separate conductor's book includes continuity information and suggested formations illustrated by line drawing. Conductor $1.00, band books 40¢. The shows include:

"First Game Show"
"Country Capers"
"Our American Heritage"
"Sports through the Seasons'
"Toys Come to Life"
"Readin, Ritin, and Rithmetic
"Thanksgiving Show"
"Flag Ceremony"

Prescott-Pronk-Wenger, "The Band Pageant and Maneuver Series", Schmitt Publications, Minneapolis, Minn., 1940 (No. 1); 1941 (No. 2, 3, 4).

Four pageants for outdoor use that can be adapted for stage or basketball floor. Instrumentation and charts for small (48), medium (72), or large (124) band. Musical numbers and charts are shown with directions for rehearsal and performance in the director's part $2.50. Titles include:

"Gay 90 Revue"
"Down on the Farm"
"American Flag Parade"
"Uncle Sam in Revue"

Rasch, Harold, "Mini-book of Polkas", Hal Leonard, Winona, Minn., 1953.

March size printed on card stock for use in lyres with complete procedure chart for each player. These are short episodes and can easily be included in a full presentation. Conductor 50¢, parts 15¢. Titles include:

"Tinker Polka"
"Rain Rain Polka"
"Village Tavern Polka"
"Springtime Polka"

Rasch, Harold, "Mini-book of Headliner Marches", Hal Leonard, Winona, Minn., 1953.

March size printed on card stock for use in lyres with complete procedure chart for each player. These are short episodes and can easily be included in a full length presentation. Conductor 50¢, parts 15¢. Titles include:

"The Porecaster"
"The Admiral"
"Color Guard"
"Esprite de Corps"

Schinstine-Hoey, "Drum Cadences for All Occasions", Southern, San Antonio, Texas 1953.

Excellent for young bands. Only six rudiments are used throughout the cadences in this little book. 60¢.

Schinstine-Hoey, "40 New Street Cadences", Southern, San Antonio, Texas, 1953.

Cadences of original and novelty type. Roll-off signals, duet and trio cadences .75¢.

Spicer, Randall, "Field Formation Series" Big 3 (Feist, Miller, Robbins), N.Y., 1949 and later.

Single number for band in standard arrangements. Each set of parts includes an octavo sheet in the conductor's part charting the formation for a 60-piece band. Spicer has designed an appropiate and clear formation for each title. The reverse of the chart sheet outlines the rehearsal and performance suggestions. Band arrangements are made by selected composers. Titles issued to date include the following:

trombone	"Darktown Strutter's Ball"
star on stairs	"Stairway to the Stars"
sleigh	"Santa Claus Is Coming to Town"
rickshaw	"China Boy"
rainbow	"Over the Rainbow"
stick horse	"Horse A-Piece Medley"
girl	"Alice Blue Gown"
drum	"Drums in My Heart"
trumpet and note	"Blow the Blues Medley"
moon	"Blue Moon"
heart	"I'll See You in My Dreams"
saxophone	"Goofus"

star	"National Emblem"
note and lyre	"Swing Medley"
	"Stompin at the Savoy"
	"Sing, Sing, Sing'¹
Eiffel tower	"Waltz Medley"
	"Diane"
	"Charmaine"
tulip	"When You Wore a Tulip"
bulldog	"Yale Boola"
Uncle Sam hat	"Yankee Doodle Polka"
three leaf clover	"Peg O' My Heart"
moon over mountain	"Springtime in the Rockies"
quarter moon	"Blue Moon"
ukulele	"Hawaiian War Chant"
girl in bonnet	"K-K-K-Katy"
man and pipe	"Great Day for the Irish"
rose	"Moonlight and Roses"
cowboy hat	"I'm an Old Cowhand"
heart and arrow	"The Waltz You Saved for Me"
anchor	"Anchors Aweigh"
tiger head	"Tiger Rag"
lamb head	"Whiffenpoof Song"
locomotive	"Chattanooga Choo Choo"
marching stick figure	"South Rampart Street Parade"
stick figure (flapper girl)	"Josephine"
ranger with gun	"Rangers Song"
sun rising	"Day Break"
stick figure (football player)	"Feist Football Medley"

Tarver, James L., "Swing Fanfares", Fillmore (C. Fischer), New York City, 1951.

Twelve (12) swing and legitimate fanfares. Also some band cheers and pep items.

Traver-Irons, "The Old Woman Who Lived in a Shoe", Victor, Dallas, Texas, 1946.

Single band number. Conductor's part contains complete directions for rehearsal and performance together with script and charts. Duration about 9 minutes.

Thomas, Max, "Show Medleys", Kjos, Park Ridge, 1950.

Single issues of medleys of three or four short tunes which can be used separately or together as the nucleus for a complete show. Good sounding, easy arrangements a la Paul Yoder. $2.00 each. Titles include:

"Cowboy Capers"
"Manhattan Medley"

Walters, Harold, "Dance Time Band Book", Rubank, Chicago, 1954.

Trick steps and moving routines for use with low bleachers or street parades. Conductor $1.25, band books 40¢. Show titles include:

"Circus Show"
"Sweetheart Show"
"Dixie Show"
"Latin American Show"

Walters, Harold, "Folk Songs and Ballads for Band", Rubank, Chicago 1955.

This is an excellent source of music for the half-time formations. Arrangements are easy in grade using standard instrumentation. Some of the titles include:

"Big Rocky Candy Mountain"
"Charlie Is My Darlin' "
"Clementine"
"Dear Evelina"
"Down in the Valley"
"Flow Gently, Sweet Afton"
"Hot Time in the Old Town Tonight"
"Kentucky Babe"
"Little David, Play on Your Harp"
"Over the River and through the Woods"
"Lonesome Road"
"Volga Boatman"

Walters, Harold, "O. K. March Folio", Rubank, Chicago, 1951.

Sixteen marches with a modern flavor in moderately easy and intermediate grade. These marches are arranged in standard instrumentation and are excellent for football and basketball use. Conductor $1.25, band books 40¢. Some sample titles include:

"Burst of Trumpets"
"Dixieland Revel"
"Latin Americana"
"Redskin Ramble"

Walters, Harold, "Short and Snappy", Rubank, Chicago, 1951.

A collection of thirty tunes written with the short football or basketball time-out

in mind. The standard instrumentation and solid arrangements are intermediate grade of difficulty. Conductor $1.00, band books 40¢. Some sample titles include:

"Bleacher Boogie"
"Gridiron Polka"
"Mambo Time"
"Sixty Seconds Samba"
"Pre-Game Salute"
"Post Game Polka"
six fanfares

Walters, Harold, "Thirty-Two Marchettes", Rubank, Chicago, 1954.

Thirty-two short extractions from famous and standard marches by Sousa, Hall, Chambers, and others. Marches have solid arrangements with standard instrumentation. Most of the numbers are 32 bars long, repeated, and are written for specific use at sport events. Arrangements are also excellent for marching band use. Conductor $1.00, band books 40¢.

Warrington, John, "Marching in Swingtime", Big 3, New York City, 1955.

Fifteen old standard tunes often used on the football field in a quickstep size book. Conductor (octavo) $1.00, parts 50¢. All tunes are in marchtime. Sample titles include:

"Diane"
"Toot, Toot, Tootsie"
"All I Do Is Dream of You"
"China Boy"
"Patriots' Parade"
"Side Shows"
"Sing Session"
"Sob Sisters"
"Travel Time"

Wettlaufer, J. Maynard, "Marching Band Series", Shapiro-Bernstein and Co., N.Y. 1948 and later.

Single band numbers are arranged in traditional scoring with formations charted by Dr. Wettlaufer for a 60 piece band. Charts show placement of twirlers, basses, drums, and drum majors in the formations for best effect. Conductor's part includes a sheet giving suggested rehearsal and performance procedures for each formation. FB $1.50, SB $2.00. Titles issued to date include the following:

Titles issued to date include the following:

barrel	"Beer Barrel Polka"
clarinet	"Way Down Yonder in New Orleans"
wheel	"Wagon Wheels"

Wettlaufer-Mills-Lang, "Mills Field Formation Band Series", Mills, N.Y., 1948 and later.

Single numbers to be purchased separately. Each title has two field formations charted by Wettlaufer and Mills with arrangements by Lang in the simplified two voice division (only 10 different band parts). This makes it possible to use the faster cadences if desired. Titles issued to date include the following:

"America I Love You"
"Blue Skirt Waltz"
"Dinah"
"Down by the Station"
"Let a Smile Be Your Umbrella"
"Let's All Sing Like the Birdies Sing"
"Mary Lou"
"Rock-A-Bye Your Baby With a Dixie Melody"

Yoder, Paul, "Band Shows No. 1", Kjos, Park Ridge, 1942.

Seven complete half-time shows, seven band cheers, and a flag raising ceremony which are adaptable for indoor use in an assembly or basketball game. Conductor $1.50, band books 40¢. Show titles include:

"America on Parade"
"Minstrel Jubilee"
"Ship Ahoy"
"Homecoming"
"Shoulder Arms"
"County Fair"
"Good Neighbors"

Yoder, Paul, "Band Shows No. 2", Kjos, Park Ridge, 1943.

Six complete half-time shows including four to six formations together with rehearsal and production instructions for each show. Formations are indicated by line drawings. No charts. Music is well arranged in an easy grade. Chorus parts are available for all shows for assembly presentation. Conductor $1.00, band books 40¢.

"Guess Conductor"
"Cavalcade of United Nations"
"Defenders of Liberty"
"Travelogue"
"American Thanksgiving"
"The Christmas Story"

Yoder, Paul, "Big Ten Band Books", Kjos, Park Ridge, 1953.

Sixteen recent pop tunes in easy arrangements. Dance step routines for each tune are written by Stefan Jones of Miami, Florida. Many of the tunes also have suggested formations. Conductor, $1.00; Conductor Drill Book, $1.00; parts, 40¢; Student Drill Book, 40¢. Sample titles include:

"It Takes Two To Tango"
"Jambalaya"

Yoder, Paul, "Football Revues", Kjos, Park Ridge, 1946.

Eight half-time shows scored within the grade II or III (easy) range. Conductor's book contains suggested routines and formations, but no charts. Formations are illustrated by line drawing. Conductor $1.00, band books 40¢. Show titles include:

"Pre-Game Salute"
"Music in the Air"
"Hat Parade"
"At the Circus"
"Drum Major's Dilemma"
"Moonlight Romance"
"Two-Band Revue"
"Precision Drill"

Yoder, Paul, "Grand Stand", Kjos, Park Ridge, 1951.

A book of six half-time shows and a set of fanfares for football field use. Formations are illustrated by line drawings. No charts, music solidly arranged. Conductor $1.50, band books 40¢. Show titles include:

"Patriotic Salute"
"Television Revue"
"New York Holiday"

"Southern Style"
"It's Your Home Town"
"Day Dream"
"Dress Parade"
"Meet the Classes"
"Football Fanfares"

Yoder, Paul, "Pigskin Pageants", Kjos, Park Ridge, 1949.

Seven half-time shows in book form. Six fanfares and two school songs included. Some titles are published separately. Conductor $1.50, band books 40¢. Titles include:

"Halloween"
"Sports Calendar"
"Touchdown Parade"
"Swing Shift"
"Old McDonald's Band"
"Frontier Days"
"Childhood Memories"

Yoder, Paul, "Series Sixty Band Shows", Kjos, Park Ridge, 1945 and later.

Shows are published separately. Many are included in Yoder's Band Show Books. Well arranged for marching band, 60 parts per set on a double page. Each show is complete with fanfares, music, and routines. $2.75 per set. Titles include:

"Minstrel Jubilee"
"Ship Ahoy!"

"Homecoming"
"County Fair"
"Travelogue"
"Music in the Air"
"Hat Parade"
"At the Circus"
"Drum Major's Dilemma"
"Moonlight Romance"
"Sports Calendar"
"Halloween"
"Childhood Memories"
"Old McDonald's Band"

Yoder, Paul, "Sound-Off", Shapiro Bernstein, N.Y., 1951.

A band arrangement by Paul Yoder of the "Duckworth Chant" with precision marching instructions for show. FB $1.50, SB $2.00.

Yoder, Paul, "Stunt Band Folio", Rubank, Chicago, 1934.

Sixteen numbers adaptable for football or basketball use. Some excellent ideas here. Conductor 60¢, band books 40¢.

Yoder-Cheyette, "Down the Gridiron" and "Touchdown", Fox, N.Y., 1947.

Two numbers with arrangements by Paul Yoder and football and goalpost formations charted by Irving Cheyette. $2.00.

CHAPTER VII

MARCHING BAND TRAINING MATERIALS

Annotated Bibliography

Benner - Painter, "The Art of Baton Spinning", Gamble, Chicago, 1942, Vol. I (elementary), Vol. II (intermediate).

Excellent for preparation of twirlers for contests using the MENC - NIMAC (NSBOVA) judging sheets.

Bennett, George T., "Field Routines for Marching Band Contests and Public Exhibitions", Gamble, Chicago, 1938.

Five show ideas. Four routines for use at football games and one specifically laid out for use on the baseball field. Vol. VI in the Marching Maneuver Series.

Bennett, George T., "Grooming the Marching Band for High School Contests", Gamble, Chicago, 1937.

Vol. III of the Marching Maneuver Series. A "must" for band directors who enter their bands in marching contest-festivals.

Bennett, George T., "Required and Special Maneuvers for High School Marching Band Contests", Gamble, Chicago, 1937.

Vol. IV in the Marching Maneuver Series. The title is self-explanatory.

Bennett, George T., "Street Routines for Marching Band Contests and Public Exhibitions", Gamble, Chicago, 1938.

Five routines that can be easily adapted to one's own band. Vol. V in the Marching Maneuver Series.

Bennett, George T., "The 'In' and 'Out' of Twenty-six Letter Formations", Gamble, Chicago, 1939.

Directors can pick up some good pointers from the charts in this book. Vol. IX in the Marching Maneuver Series.

Bennett - Whitfield, "New and Novel Formations for Marching Bands and Drum Corps", Gamble, Chicago, 1938.

Precision marching routines only. Vol. VII in the Marching Maneuver Series.

Bergen, Hal, "Band Pageantry", Remick, N.Y., 1948, Conductor $1.50, Parts $ .40 each.

Five half-time field shows together with an excellent section on "Building the Football Band", and other sections on the organization and preparation of the marching band. Show titles include:

"Patriotic Pageant"
"Transportation Pageant"
"Western Pageant"
"Football Pageant"
"When Day Is Done"

Bird, George "Red", "Football Band Show Chart Forms", Mills, New York, 1946.

Spiral band books of 24 football field charts, graphed for 30" steps. Three music staffs of music at top of each chart for scoring music cues.

Black - Benner, "Fourteen Characteristic Tricks for the Baton", Gamble, Chicago, 1942.

No text — all pictures in the "movie camera action" technique. Many unusual and not too well known tricks presented.

Booth, Gaedke, Miller, "Baton Twirling", Ludwig Drum Co., Chicago.

The book is profusely illustrated. Single tricks for the beginner and advanced twirls for the solo twirler. Very complete.

Brodt Music Co., "Music for the Marching Band", Brodt Pub. Co., Charlotte, N.C.

A very complete list of materials for the marching band.

Burford, Cary Clive, "We're Loyal to You, Illinois", Interstate, Danville, Ill., 1952. Part 13, Chapters 31, 32, 33.

Three chapters on football pageantry at the University of Illinois which include a number of pictures of the Illinois Band in football field formations.

Cecil, Herbert M., "Fundamental Principals of the Organization, Management, and Teaching of the School Band", Eastman School of Music, Rochester, N.Y., 1953.

Clark, "Selmer Twirl-A-Flag Manual", H. Selmer Co., Elkhart Ind. 1945.

Cuthbert, Donald, "Maneuva - Band Manual", Maneuva - Band, Beloit, Wisconsin, 1950.

Instructions and suggestions on using miniature scaled bandsmen on a scale chart of the football field. Numerous formations are pictured or in line drawings.

Dale, Carroll R., "Fundamentals of Drill", Gamble, Chicago, 1942.

Good ideas for basic drill maneuvers and for those first drills with the new band each fall. Well - illustrated with pictures and diagrams.

DeVita, Ray "Standard Dance Music Guide", DeVita, 150 Knickerbocker Ave., Brooklyn, New York, 1954.

A very complete listing of thousands of pep tunes, show tunes, and old standards. Title only, plus starting note and key. Annual supplements keep it up to date. An invaluable aid to the director looking for show ideas.

Duncan, C. J., "Beginner's Baton Book", Gamble, Chicago, 1942.

Elementary instruction for baton twirlers. The "movie camera action" pictures contained in this book are a great aid to the beginner.

Dvorak, R. F., "Band on Parade", Carl Fischer, New York, 1937.

Excellent text material and profusely illustrated with pictures. Covers every detail of good marching band fundamentals. Divided into the following sections.

"Musical Performance"
"The Band Formation"
"School of the Bandsmen"
"Drum Major and Drum Section"
"Band Maneuvers"
"Planning Special Maneuvers"
"Special Formations"
"Twirling the Baton"

"New York Holiday"
"Southern Style"
"Day Dreams"
"Political Parade"
"Shoulder Arms"
"Precision Drill"

Dykema-Gehrkens, "High School Music", Birchard, Boston, 1941, 614 pp. Sec. p. 147 ff.

Elkhart Inst. Co., "The Fundamentals of Training a Good Marching Band", Elkhart Band Instrument Co., Elkhart, Indiana, 1940.

Hackney - Emerson, "Parade Stunts", Gamble, Chicago, 1941.

Some good suggestions to help the director liven up the next parade appearance. Vol. X in the Marching Maneuver Series.

Hackney - McCord, "Novel Drills and Formations for Basketball Games, Gamble, Chicago, 1939.

One of the best for basketball floor ideas. Vol. VIII in the Marching Maneuver Series.

Haug, Leonard H., "Gridiron Work Sheet", Schmitt, Minneapolis, 1954.

A pad of 50 work sheets (letter size) for laying out formations and movements 8 steps to 5 yards. Covers the field between the 25 yard lines.

Hindsley, Mark, "Band, Attention", Gamble, Chicago 1932.

Hindsley, Mark, "How to Twirl a Baton", Ludwig Drum Co., Chicago, 1930.

Hindsley, Mark, "Some Aspects of the Marching Band", MENC Yearbook, 1934, p. 188.

Hindsley, Mark, "Twenty-Four Formations, Designs, and Entrances for the Marching Band", Gamble, Chicago, 1935.

Vol. I in the Marching Maneuver Series. The title is self explanitory.

Johnston, Lawrence, "Parade Techniques" Belwin, Rockville Centre, L.I., N.Y.,1944.

A method book for parading a coordi-

University of Florida "Gator" Band, Gainesville, Florida
Harold Bachman, Director. Saxophone and Blue Note Formation

nated marching band, twirling corps, and color guard, containing seventy-three illustrations and charts.

Jones, L. Bruce, "Building the Instrumental Music Department", Carl Fischer, N.Y., 1949, Chapter XX.

Kjos, Neil, "The Marching Band", MENC Yearbook, 1931, p. 184.

Lang, Phillip, "Scoring for the Band", Mills N.Y., 1950, p. 187 ff.

Lee, Jack, "Marching Band Techniques", Hal Leonard, Winona, Minn., 1955.

A complete textbook and reference for the director who wants to develop a first rate marching and show band.

Lee, Jack, "Modern Marching Band Techniques", Hal Leonard, Winona, Minn., 1955, $5.00.

A well - organized and quite complete book on the marching band. Many ideas for shows and field formations. Good line drawings to illustrate the fundamentals of drill. A listing of some of the chapter headings will indicate the breadth and scope of this work

"Educational Value of the Marching Band"
"Administration of the Marching Band"
"Conceiving Ideas"
"Timing the Band Show"
"Charting the Football Band"
"Basic Block Band Maneuvers"
"Drill the Bandsman"
"Cadence"
"Dance Steps"
"Percussion"
"Uniforms"
"The Drum Major"
"The Director"

Leonard, Hal, "Band Shows Can Be Easy", Hal Leonard, Winona, Minn., 1948.

Entrance formalities, letter formations, building the show from formula, ideas for night games, music and drum beats and a complete homecoming show are included.

Long, A. H., "Marching to the Yard Lines", Luther Music Co., Ponca City, Okla., 1952.

Explains procedures used when marching to the yardlines. Good foot placement diagrams. Also more than a hundred field formation suggestions illustrated with line drawings.

Ludwig, William, "The Art of Swiss Flag Twirling", Ludwig Drum Co., Chicago, 194 .

Elementary instructions and fundamentals of Flag Swinging. Excellent illustrations. Students can use this book with a minimum of private instruction.

McAllister-Bennett, "An Interpretation of National High School Competition Requirements", Gamble, Chicago, 1942.

Nine of the National High School Twirling Competition Requirements are carefully outlined and supported by training material.

Mahan, Jack H., "Quick-Steps to Marching", Carl Fischer, N.Y., 1953.

A pocket size book to be used either by the director or as a text in the hands of students. It is a complete and easy to understand explanation of the elements of marching. Sections include:

"Commands"
"Stationary Positions for the Individual"
"Marching Positions for the Individual"
"Marching Positions for the Organization"
"Marching Maneuvers for the Organization"
"Preparation for Inspection"

Malstrom, George N., "The Drum Major's Manual", Ludwig Drum Co., Chicago, Ill., 1943.

A well illustrated book that contains basic Drum Major positions, signals, and duties.

Mills-Wettlaufer, "Show Band Perspective

Plotting Chart and Handbook", Mills, N.Y., 194 . 10 Charts and Handbook $5.00, Extra Charts, $2.50 for 10.

Chart forms for use when plotting with

perspective to make the formations easier to recognize particularly by spectators in low bleachers.

Oldfield, Willis P., "Twenty and Seven Drill Band Maneuvers", Mills, N.Y.

Director's Manual and Student's Guide published separately. All letters of the alphabet are included together with entrances and exits. This is a very popular book.

Opsahl, Julian E., "Steps and Maneuvers for the Marching Band", Instrumentalist, Evanston, Ill., 1954.

The fundamentals of marching, 44 steps and movements, developing a superior show band, and various maneuvers. Illustrated in detail.

Painter - Benner, "The Underhand Techniques of Baton Twirling", Gamble, Chicago, 1942.

Good illustrations of the Vamp, Cartwheel, etc., using the French Technique by means of the "movie camera action" pictures.

Righter, Charles B.,"Gridiron Pageantry", Carl Fischer, N.Y., 1941.

Roberts, Bob, "The Twirler and the Twirling Corps", Carl Fischer, N.Y., 1954.

Step-by-step text enables a director with a very limited knowledge of twirling to organize and develop a twirling corps or solo twirlers. The excellent illustrations are by Nadine Whalen.

University of Illinois Marching Band, Urbana, Illinois
Mark Hindsley, Director. Outline of United States for "Get Out the Vote" Show

131

Rohner, Traugott, "Football Maneuver Chart", Instrumentalist, Evanston, Ill., 1947.

Charts about 10" x 31" laid out graph style.

Savage-Painter, "Six Football Programs", Gamble, Chicago, 1943.

Six excellent football shows are completely worked out with script and prop cues. There are alternate routines for night or daytime use as well as routines adaptable for basketball and street use.

Schilling, Richard, "Colored-Light Band Formations", Gamble, Chicago, 1949.

"Twenty 'Color Pictures' for Night Games and Festivities". Charts are well worked out with some suitable for small band and low bleachers. Good introductory chapter on care and use of band lights is included.

Schilling, Richard L., "Marching Band Maneuvers", Instrumentalist, Evanston, Ill., 1952.

Literally hundreds of show ideas, each illustrated by line drawings or photographs are classified under the following headings:

"Half-Time Shows and Pageants"
"Stunts and Novelties"
"Formations and Stunts Adaptable
    to Low Bleachers"
"Entrances, Drills, and Maneuvers"
"Formations and Drills Using Lights"

Included also are sections on microphone, sound effects, and use of colored flames.

Schilling, Richard L., "New Formations and Materials for the Marching Band", Instrumentalist, Evanston, Ill., 1948.

Forty or more half-time show ideas contributed as "my best" by outstanding high school directors throughout the U.S. The book is profusely illustrated by line drawings leaving details to be worked out by the local director.

Selected Authors, "Marching Maneuver Series", 10 Volumes, Gamble, Chicago, 1937 and 1938.

Vol. I — "24 Formations, Designs and
    Entrances"
Vol. II — "Practical Stunts and Evolutions"
Vol. III — "Grooming the Band for High
    School Contests"
Vol. IV — "Required Movements and
    Special Maneuvers"
Vol. V — "Street Routines for Contests
    and Exhibitions"
Vol. VI — "Field Routines for Contests"
Vol. VII — "New and Novel Formations"
Vol. VIII — "Drills for Basketball Floorshows"
Vol. IX — "The In and Out of 26 Letter
    Formations"
Vol. X — "Parade Stunts"

Smith-Capel, "Practical Stunts and Evolutions", Gamble, Chicago, 1935.

Volume II in the Marching Maneuver Series. Good ideas for field or street use.

Tatgenhorst - Wolf, "Precision Marching with the Band", Bourne, N.Y., 1954.

Six precision drill shows and several entrances and exits are well charted with suggested list of music titles. Informative chapters include:

"The Reason for Precision Marching"
"The Rehearsal"
"Organization of the Marching Band"
"Incidental but Important Information"

West, Adam, "Marching Class Method", Southern Music, San Antonio, Texas, 1953. Separate Director and Student Manuals.

A marching band method book. The material is divided into twenty sections — one for each marching day. It is an important contribution to the limited material available for marching band instruction.

Wettlaufer, Maynard J., "Building a Band Show", Belwin, Rockville Centre, N.Y., 1948.

A complete practical treatment of the entire marching band area with sections on publicity, uniforms, transportation, and other details.

Wilcoxon, Charles, "The Drummer on Parade", Wilcoxon's Drum Shop, 1947.

Fifty street beats for drum sections.

Wilson, Harry R., "Music in the High School," Silver Burdett, N.Y., 1941, p. 187 ff.

White, William Carter, "A History of Military Music in America", C. Fischer, New York, 1944.

A fine source of background information of American band music from Continental Army days to the present. The more than 70 photographs are of real historical value.

Yoder, Paul, "Arranging Method for School Bands", Big 3, New York.

A complete text to help the director who must, or chooses to, make his own arrangements for band shows. Many examples to illustrate points discussed. An outstanding book on arranging.